^{The}Art of Total Relevance

Laurence Perrine
Southern Methodist University

NEWBURY HOUSE PUBLISHERS, Inc. / Rowley / Massachusetts

Library of Congress Cataloging in Publication Data

Perrine, Laurence.
The art of total relevance.

Bibliography: p.
1. Poetry--Addresses, essays, lectures. I. Title.
PN1055.P39   808.1   76-1978
ISBN 0-88377-055-5

NEWBURY HOUSE PUBLISHERS, Inc.

Language Science
Language Teaching
Language Learning

68 Middle Road, Rowley, Massachusetts 01969

Printed in the U.S.A.   First printing: September 1976
                                              5 4 3 2 1

Preface

The essays which follow were written by a teacher and lover of poetry. They were prepared for different audiences—some for students, some for general readers, some for fellow teachers—but all, I hope, will have an interest for the general reader with an interest in poetry. Each essay was written for its own occasion, and therefore, though the essays touch on various aspects of poetry, there is no attempt at a grand design. I have grouped them, however, into three sections. The first has mainly to do with problems of reading and interpretation, or the poem in relation to itself. The second deals with problems of evaluation, or the poem in relation to other poems. The third treats problems of significance, or poetry in relation to other human concerns.

Southern Methodist University   Laurence Perrine
Dallas, Texas
January 1, 1976

Acknowledgments
and Permissions

COVER   The cover photograph of *Echinarachnius parma* is furnished by courtesy of the Peabody Museum of Salem (Massachusetts). Photo by M. W. Sexton. The cover type design is by L. J. Kordaszewski.

CALIFORNIA ENGLISH JOURNAL   for "Interpreting Poetry—Two Ways of Going Wrong" from Volume 1, No. 1 (Winter 1965). © California Association of Teachers of English. Reprinted by permission.

JONATHAN CAPE, LTD and MRS. H. M. DAVIES   for "The Example" from *The Complete Poems of W. H. Davies.* Reprinted by permission.

COLBY LIBRARY QUARTERLY   for "A Reading of 'Miniver Cheevy'." © June 1962. Reprinted by permission.

THE COLLEGE ENGLISH ASSOCIATION, INC.   for "The Art of Total Relevance," from *The CEA Critic* (Nov. 1973) and "But Deliver Us from Evil" from *The CEA Critic* (Dec. 1967). Reprinted by permission.

HARCOURT BRACE JOVANOVICH, INC.   for "Rhythm and Meter" from *Poetry: A Closer Look* by James M. Reid, John Ciardi, and Laurence Perrine. © 1963 by Harcourt Brace Jovanovich, Inc. and reprinted with their permission. For "if everything happens that can't be done." Copyright, 1944, by E. E. Cummings; renewed, 1972, by Nancy Andrews. Reprinted from *Complete Poems 1913-1962* by E. E. Cummings by permission of Harcourt Brace Jovanovich, Inc.

HARPER & ROW, PUBLISHERS, INC.   for "Two butterflies went out at noon" (poem #131) and "The snow that never drifts" (poem #49) from *Bolts of Melody* by Emily Dickinson, edited by Mabel Loomis Todd and Millicent Todd Bingham. Copyright 1945 by The Trustees of Amherst College. By permission of Harper & Row, Publishers, Inc.

HOLT RINEHART AND WINSTON, INC.   for "A Patch of Old Snow" and "A Prayer in Spring" from *The Poetry of Robert Frost,* edited by Edward Connery Lathem. Copyright 1916, 1934, © 1969 by Holt, Rinehart and Winston, Inc. Copyright 1944, © 1962 by Robert Frost. Reprinted by permission of Holt, Rinehart and Winston, Inc. For "On moonlit heath and lonesome bank" and "The Immortal Part" from "A Shropshire Lad"—Authorized Edition—from *The Collected Poems of A. E. Housman.* Copyright 1939, 1940, © 1965 by Holt, Rinehart and Winston, Inc. Copyright © 1967, 1968 by Robert E. Symons. Reprinted by permission of Holt, Rinehart and Winston, Inc.

HOUGHTON MIFFLIN COMPANY   for "Wind and Silver" from *The Complete Poetical Works of Amy Lowell.* Reprinted by permission of the publisher.

Contents

The Art of Total Relevance

Part One

The Poem
in Relation
to Itself

The Art of Total Relevance

Attempting to define poetry is one of the more popular parlor games. Is it also one of the more futile? Certainly, if all the definitions that have been produced were laid end to end, the result would be longer than *The Faerie Queene* and would not rhyme so well. And like *The Faerie Queene*, it would still be unfinished. There are some, indeed, who claim that poetry is undefinable. "Poetry," writes Herbert Read, "is properly speaking a transcendental quality—a sudden transformation which words assume under a particular influence—and we can no more define this quality than we can define a state of grace." And Edwin Arlington Robinson has said, "Poetry has two characteristics. One is that it is, after all, undefinable. The other is that it is eventually unmistakable."

Can poetry be defined? Or is the attempt to do so futile? I am not sure whether poetry can be defined; but I am sure that attempts to define it are not futile. There are, after all, two kinds of definitions. Using my own nomenclature, I call them scientific definitions and poetic definitions. Scientific definitions are *real* definitions. They attempt to draw limits around a word, to pin it down, to clean and stuff it for the dictionary. Though they serve a utilitarian purpose, they frequently have to kill the word before they can lay it out. Poetic definitions, on the other hand, are not really definitions at all. Instead of trying to establish boundaries, they seek to knock a hole into the infinite. They are suggestive, not definitive. But they have this advantage: They catch the bird on the wing. They do not cage it, to be sure. But they do set it flying in the sky of the imagination.

Poetic definitions, in short, are half-truths or untruths which work in the service of truth. Everyone has heard the famous definition of a camel: "A camel is a horse made by a committee." Not of much use to a dictionary-maker, to be sure, or to a systematic zoologist, but of considerable value to the rest of us, though it perhaps tells us more about committees than about camels. Then, there is a definition of marriage which I cherish: "Marriage is giving half your food away to get the other half cooked." An unromantic and incomplete definition, to be sure; but a healthy corrective to more idealistic definitions.

Perhaps the trouble with a scientific definition of poetry is that it does attempt the impossible. The very notion of a scientific definition of poetry suggests a contradiction. If it takes a crook to catch a crook, perhaps it takes a poet to define poetry. At any rate, one may get valuable insights from poetic definitions that won't bear up under logical scrutiny. "Poetry," writes W. H. Auden, "might be defined as the clear expression of mixed feelings." It's a definition that won't apply to all poems, I fear, but what a helpful insight it gives into others! "Poetry," says Robert Frost, "is what evaporates from all translations." Here poetry, apparently, is not the whole house of a poem, but some sort of perfume, or essence, or ghost that inhabits it. But again, what a lovely insight! And there are many others: In Lascelles Abercrombie's words, "The art of poetry is simply the art of electrifying language with extraordinary meaning." In R. P. Blackmur's "Poetry is life framed and identified." In Robert Frost's (again), poetry is "words that have become deeds." Not that all poetic definitions are equally satisfactory. A few I would eagerly throw into the ashcan. Such as this one by Grant Allen: "A poem consists of all the purest and most beautiful elements in the poet's nature, crystallized into the aptest and most exquisite language, and adorned with all the outer embellishment of musical cadence or dainty rhyme." Or this one by Alfred Austin: "Poetry is . . . the transfiguration of the Actual or Real into the Ideal, at a lofty elevation, through the medium of melodious or nobly sounding verse." Such definitions make poetry the dainty lace embroidery on the Muse's underwear, not the Muse herself. The Muse, I submit, is not an ethereal, bloodless, maiden lady, all spirit and no body. She sweats; she knows anger; and her thoughts are not always chaste. All those who define poetry in terms too dainty or too exquisite or too lofty I would sentence to reading Carl Sandburg's *Chicago*, "Hog Butcher for the World" until they die or repent.

But defining poetry is a game that all may play. I should like to define poetry, myself, as *the art of the totally relevant*. A successful poem is a verbal construct of which every part has manifold relations to every other part, and of which no part could be changed or shifted without weakening the whole. Not only is every part relevant to the meaning of the whole, it is totally relevant: That is, it is held in its place in the poem not by one bond only, like a picture hanging from a nail, but by many bonds, like the solar system. Every word, every image, every rhyme, every accent has its purpose and function in the totally relevant poem. There is a reason for its being as it is and not otherwise, and that reason can be explained.

You see at once how defective my definition is as a scientific definition. First of all, you point out, this condition of total relevance is an ideal condition which no human construct ever actually achieves. Poems are human creations, made by imperfect human beings out of imperfect human materials. They exist on earth, not in heaven, not in Plato's realm of ideal forms. Granted; and I should have to revamp my definition to: "Poetry is the art of *almost* total relevance." But, you protest, this definition might apply to music or to painting as much as it does to poetry. Granted again, I grudgingly concede, and retreat another step. Total relevance is the condition to which all art aspires. But before you make me back down further, let me develop my idea, and see if there is not some value in it.

Poetry, I contend, is a verbal art in which every part has an extraordinary relevance, that is, an extraordinary number of reasons for being what it is and where it is. Other forms of language lack this extraordinary relevance. Take algebraic language, for example. The truths of algebra are almost independent of the language they are expressed in. An algebraic statement, such as $x^2 + 16x = 32$, may be expressed in an almost infinite number of ways without suffering in meaning or being made less useful or less valid. We can state it backward: $32 = 16x + x^2$. We can transpose any term to the other side of the *equals* sign: $x^2 + 16x - 32 = 0$. We can replace all of the terms by equivalents: $x \cdot x + 4^2 x = 4 \cdot 8$. Or: $\dfrac{2x^2}{2} + (12 + 4)x = 4(6 + 2)$. The possibilities are literally infinite. We can even change the x to y or z so long as we preserve our understanding of what it stands for.

Or take ordinary language. "It is now 3:45 P.M.," we say, or "It is now 3:45 in the afternoon," or perhaps "It is at present a quarter to four" or "It's fifteen minutes to four" or "It's forty-five minutes after three." It makes little difference how we say it, for no word has enough relevance to make it indispensable either where it is or any place else. We may even translate it into French, "C'est trois heures quarante-cinq" or into German, "Es ist ein Viertel vor vier," and, at least if we're speaking to the right people, no one will care.

Lawyers are much concerned with precision of language; but do they really care about the difference between "Spitting on busses is forbidden by law" and "The law forbids spitting on busses"? Indeed, are they not just as likely to refer to spitting as "expectoration" or to call busses "public conveyances" or "public carriers"?

When we come to poetry, we move in a different world. Here all is ordered, adjusted, made relevant. The words spin in their courses, held in place by subtle ties of gravity, speed, and motion, and we cannot change one without upsetting their whole universe. Take, for example, the opening line of Tennyson's *The Lotos-Eaters*, in which Ulysses urges on his men: "'Courage,' he said, and pointed toward the land." Can we turn this around, like the algebraic statement? Let's try. "He said, 'Courage,' and pointed toward the land." The words are exactly the same, but half the courage has drained out of them. The challenge no longer rings out like a bugle on the air, and Ulysses' men, we should guess, no longer respond by bending their backs to the oar with redoubled vigor. For, as Tennyson wrote it, the word "courage" is given extraordinary energy both by its position in the sentence and by its metrical isolation. As every student knows, or should know, the beginning and the end of a sentence are the most important positions for emphasis. Tennyson puts his important word in the important part of the sentence. But Tennyson goes further, and makes the meter relevant too. The strong accent on the initial syllable of "courage" is followed by two unaccented syllables, then by an only lightly accented "said," followed by another unaccented syllable; not until we come to "pointed" do we run into another strong accent. This metrical isolation gives the word "courage" extraordinary emphasis, making it mean, indeed, exactly what it says. If we change the order of the words, the accent on "courage" is jammed up with other accents. Thus cabined and confined, it loses eminence, and Ulysses' words become tepid. Notice also that in the line as Tennyson wrote it, the three strongest accents fall on the three most important words: "Courage," "pointed," "land." Speech, action, and destination—the three are picked out and underscored by the meter and word order.

Many people think of poetry as words put in unnatural order for the sake of meter or rhyme, both of which are themselves artificial. In fact, we have the testimony of no less a person than Mr. Tony Weller, in *Pickwick Papers*. "Poetry's unnat'ral," he tells his son; "no man ever talked poetry 'cept a beadle on boxin' day, or Warren's blackin', or Rowland's oil, or some o' them low fellows." And, of course, Mr. Weller is right. If art is the opposite of nature, then poetry *is* unnatural, even when it comes, as Keats said it should come, "as naturally as the leaves to a tree." But only in second-rate poetry are words put in unnatural order only for the sake of meter or rhyme. In first-rate poetry the words are placed in the most meaningful order, whether that order be natural or unnatural. Indeed, it might not be a bad definition of poetry to call it the most meaningful words in the most meaningful order. Coleridge called it "the best words in the best order," and I don't know what he meant by "best" unless he meant "most meaningful."

Consider, for instance, a line from Robert Frost's last poem, published in *Life* shortly after his death. The poem is one of those witty meditations, in Frost's Horatian manner, on science and religion, a subject which much preoccupied him during his latter years. Specifically it takes off from man's conquest of gravity, enabling man to orbit vehicles into space—as Frost says:

Now that we've found the secret out of weight,
So we can cancel it however great.

At first sight Frost appears guilty of just that accusation which critics have brought against poetry, of putting words in unnatural order merely for the sake of meter. If Frost had written, "Now that we've found out the secret of weight," his meter would have sprawled headlong. But look again. Frost has changed the order of the words, *not* primarily for meter but for meaning. Man, in conquering gravity, has indeed found the secret *out* of weight; has extracted it, as it were; has nullified it. Thus Frost, in ordering his words, has made "out" go both with the verb that precedes and with the preposition that follows. He has doubled its relevance. At the same time, he has served his meter.

If the very order of the words in poetry is crucial, we hardly need to demonstrate that the choice of words is even more so. A spade is indeed a spade in poetry, and we cannot call it an implement for digging without either a fatal loss of meaning or a very good reason. Words in good poems do not have substitutable equivalents, as they do in "It's now 3:45 P.M." Consider, for instance, a line from Shakespeare's *Midsummer Night's Dream*. The line is a casual one, of no great import. But Shakespeare's genius shines even in his casual lines, struck off, as it were, without thought, as God mints snowflakes. This one is spoken by Theseus, Duke of Athens: "The iron tongue of midnight hath told twelve."— "The clock has struck twelve," we might have said in ordinary language; "The midnight bell has rung," or simply, "It's twelve o'clock," or "It's midnight." But Shakespeare has not merely announced the time, he has personified the midnight, has brought it to life and given it a tongue. And this is appropriate, for Theseus and his court have been enjoying the revels furnished by Bottom and his company; it will take more than a mechanical announcement to bring this festivity to an end. The midnight speaks, then, and since it speaks through a bell, it speaks with a "tongue." A different object personified might have spoken with its throat, its lips, or its voice; but the clapper of a bell is literally its tongue; so this word is relevant both to the speaker and to the bell. The tongue with which the midnight speaks is "iron." For a different hour, a different voice might have been appropriate—gold, silver, or bronze. But "iron" is relevant here both to the material of which the clapper is made and, by emotional correspondence, to the time of night. The most relevant word of all in this series, however, is the verb. "Told" is relevant first of all because of the personification. Shakespeare could have said, "The iron tongue of midnight hath *struck* twelve" or "*rung* twelve," but not without damage to the personification. On the other hand, Shakespeare could very well have preserved the personification with "said" or "spoke." But the verb "told" has a second definition meaning "counted": a bank *teller*, for example, is one who counts or tells money; and (to shift religions) one who *tells* his beads is counting on a rosary the prayers he says. Shakespeare's bell is counting the midnight hours: all twelve of them. But there is also a third meaning: "told" is a pun on the word "tolled." Thus Shakespeare, with "told" as with "tongue," is faithful both to the bell and to his personification. After all this it seems almost superfluous to point out that "tolled" is an onomatopoetic word, and that the repeated *t*'s in "tongue," "told," and "twelve" echo the repetitiveness of the *telling* and the *tolling*. These too, however, help Shakespeare approach our ideal of total relevance.

It is, in fact, this ability to use the very sound and rhythm of words as adjuncts of meaning that lifts poetry to a higher plane of relevance than the most artistic prose. The poet does not extract the nut of meaning from a word and throw the husk of sound away. Rather, like the most economical manufacturer, he utilizes both the nut and the shell—and not, like the manufacturer, separately, but together. Examine, for instance, the opening lines of Gray's *Elegy in a Country Churchyard:*

The curfew tolls the knell of parting day,
The lowing herd wind slowly o'er the lea,
The ploughman homeward plods his weary way,
And leaves the world to darkness and to me.

In the first two lines "tolls," "knell," and "lowing" are onomatopoetic: they suggest their meaning by their sound. But Gray does not leave the matter there. He reinforces the sounds of "lowing" by repeating them in "slowly," "o'er," and "lea." Both the bells and the cattle are therefore *heard* in these first two lines. Metrically, the first line is regular, echoing the regular tolling of the bells. In the second line, however, Gray does two remarkable things: first, he puts the accented word "wind" in a position normally occupied by an unaccented syllable, thus jamming three accented syllables together; second, he chooses his accented vowel sounds almost entirely from long vowels: "low," "wind," "slow," "o'er," "lea." The result of these two devices is to slow the line down, in accordance with the slow progress of the cattle. The third line metrically is the most regular of the four: the accented syllables are all very heavy, the unaccented ones very light; and this regularity is reinforced by the heavy alliteration of "ploughman" and "plod" and the secondary alliteration of "weary" and "way." The effect of this heavy regularity is to bring out the *plod:* we hear the ploughman's heavy footsteps returning wearily from labor: plod; plod; plod. In the fourth line the noteworthy feature is the very light stress on the fourth accented syllable: "and." The result of this is to require a slight compensatory pause before it in the reading, and thus to isolate the final pronoun, which introduces the speaker, and to prepare us, as does the imagery, for the meditative nature of the poem. Thus Gray makes sound, meter, and imagery all one, each relevant to the meaning and to each other.

The doctrine of total relevance needs to be illustrated, however, by a larger structure than the single line or stanza. And since heavy poetical analysis is likely to be fatiguing, I shall illustrate with a relatively light example. The poet again is Shakespeare, and the piece is the first of two lyrics, entitled *Spring* and *Winter*, with which he concluded his play *Love's Labour's Lost. Spring* is a charming but wryly humorous poem, quite relevant for ringing down the curtain on a comedy concerning sex and marriage:

When daisies pied and violets blue
    And lady-smocks all silver-white
And cuckoo-buds of yellow hue
    Do paint the meadows with delight,
The cuckoo then, on every tree,
Mocks married men; for thus sings he,
                "Cuckoo!

Cuckoo, cuckoo!" O, word of fear,
Unpleasing to a married ear!

When shepherds pipe on oaten straws,
　　And merry larks are ploughmen's clocks,
When turtles tread, and rooks, and daws,
　　And maidens bleach their summer smocks,
The cuckoo then, on every tree,
Mocks married men; for thus sings he,
　　　　　　　"Cuckoo!
Cuckoo, cuckoo!" O, word of fear,
Unpleasing to a married ear!

The poem pivots about a contrast which divides each stanza exactly in the middle. Spring is the time of flowers and birds and delight, and to this traditional aspect of spring Shakespeare yields the first four lines of each stanza. It is also the time of love; but in treating this aspect Shakespeare gives the traditional treatment of spring a wry twist. The cuckoo's note reminds the married man not only, as Tennyson points out, that "In the spring a young man's fancy lightly turns to thoughts of love," but also, less pleasing thought, that in the spring young wives are most likely to prove unfaithful. "Cuckold, cuckold!" the cuckoo seems to say to the husband by way of warning. The poem thus throws into contrast the innocent and delightful with the unpleasing or painful.

Perhaps the first thing to notice is how skillfully Shakespeare uses a figure of speech variously known as synecdoche or metonymy, the use of an aspect of an experience for the whole experience. The daisies, the violets, the lady-smocks, and the cuckoo-buds, he says, "do paint the meadows with delight." The metaphor in the verb "paint" prepares for the metonymy in the word "delight." What the flowers actually paint the meadows with, is color, but Shakespeare, by substituting the effect for which the color is the cause, makes his line doubly relevant, for it suggests both cause *and* effect. Next, by using "word" instead of *notes* for the cuckoo's call, Shakespeare prepares us to read a pun into "cuckoo" —for it is indeed the word "cuckold" which the married man fears, not the bird-notes which suggest it. And thus the poet prepares us for the second metonymy —"ear." It is the married *man*, of course, who hears the cuckoo, but Shakespeare does not call him an "ear" simply to find a rhyme for "fear." By so calling him, Shakespeare reduces him imaginatively to the one quivering, sensitive organ which will receive the insult when he is cuckolded. The figure has extraordinary relevance.

For flowers to represent the spring, Shakespeare might have chosen from a whole seed catalogue. His daisies and violets are traditional enough, and we are not surprised to find them. But why has Shakespeare chosen lady-smocks and cuckoo-buds? Why, indeed, except for their relevance, for their connections? The lady-smocks throw a connecting loop all the way into the second stanza, to the line "And maidens bleach their summer smocks," and this loop ties the two stanzas together. The cuckoo-buds also have obvious relevance: they prepare us for the cuckoobird and the implied *cuckold* which are the central subjects of the poem.

Another word, in the second stanza, demands special attention: "When turtles *tread* . . . ." Turtles, of course, are turtle-doves, and the traditional poet, writing of the innocent pleasures of spring, would have said, "When turtles *mate* . . . ." But Shakespeare uses the technical or barnyard term for the copulation of birds, and thus introduces a more earthy note. He continues: "When turtles tread, *and* rooks, *and* daws. . . ." The repeated "and's" are not there simply to fill out the meter. They have the effect of enormously magnifying the activity. The line "When turtles tread, and rooks, and daws" is not at all the same as "When rooks, daws, and turtles tread." With all this activity going on, no wonder the married man is apprehensive.

The doctrine of total relevance is incomplete unless it takes into consideration the matter of forms and stanza patterns. Can even these seemingly arbitrary patterns be made relevant in the very best poetry? Does it make any difference, really, whether a poet pours his subject matter into a sonnet, an ode, a villanelle, or a sestina? Do we not here run into the irreducibly arbitrary, the patently artificial? It would take a book to examine this problem. But let us look at how pattern works in Shakespeare's poem.

One value of pattern, like that of meter, from which it is inseparable, is that it sets up expectations from which departures are significant. The iambic tetrameter pattern with alternating rhymes that Shakespeare uses in the first four lines of each stanza is generally a tripping measure, appropriate to light and cheerful and songlike matters such as Shakespeare there treats. It is highly relevant to spring flowers and merry larks and meadows painted with delight. But in the last four lines, the pattern changes, and so does the mood. The change is signaled in the phrase "Mocks married men," where the jammed meter and the heavy alliteration inform us that the subject matter is shifting to something more solemn. The rhyme pattern also alters, shifting from alternating rhymes to rhyming couplets. The iambic tetrameter continues; but the lines now, instead of tripping along merrily, are broken up. They are broken first by the extra-metrical trochaic "Cuckoo," placed on a line by itself, thus interrupting the iambics and tetrameters and receiving a heavy emphasis relevant to its importance. Second, the pattern is broken in the following line by the ending of the sentence in the middle of the line, thus separating it into two sharply divided parts, the first half trochaic, the second half iambic. We simply *cannot read* these last four lines with the same blithe abandon with which we read the first four lines. The cuckoo's call, we might say, breaks into the stanza with the same violence with which it breaks in on the married man's peace! Shakespeare has made his pattern relevant.

Total relevance is the condition to which all art aspires. It exists absolutely, perhaps, only in heaven or in Plato's world of ideal forms. But it exists so nearly in certain symphonies, certain sculptures, certain paintings, and certain poems that we don't need to wait till we die to know what heaven is like. And for that matter, who made heaven itself if not Dante and certain other poets? I can do no better for a conclusion than to quote the concluding four lines from Richard Wilbur's poem *For the New Railway Station in Rome:*

> What is our praise or pride
> But to imagine excellence, and try to make it?
> What does it say over the door of Heaven
> But *homo fecit?*

The Nature of Proof
in the Interpretation of Poetry

That a poem may have varying interpretations is a critical commonplace. That all interpretations of a poem are equally valid is a critical heresy, but one which perennially makes its reappearance in the classroom. "Why can't a poem mean anything that a reader sees in it?" asks the student. "Why isn't one person's interpretation of a poem as good as anyone else's?" According to his theory the poem is like an inkblot in a Rorschach personality test. There are no correct or incorrect readings: there are only readings which differ more or less widely from a statistical norm.

This theory is one that poets themselves have sometimes seemed to lend support to. T. S. Eliot, in response to conjectures about the meanings of his poems, often replied, "If it suits you that way, then that is all right with me." Yeats once wrote to a friend: "I shall not trouble to make the meaning clear—a clear vivid story of a strange sort is enough. The meaning may be different with everyone." But one is not really quarreling with Eliot or Yeats in challenging this point of view. Eliot, as a critic dealing with the poetry of others, was constantly concerned with determining precise meanings. No poet, however, likes to be caught in the predicament of having to explain his own poems. He cannot say, "What I *really* meant was . . ." without admitting failure, or without saying something different (and usually much less) than what his poem said. And in doing so, he gives this diminished reading the stamp of his own authority. "A writer," E. A. Robinson once told an interviewer, "should not be his own interpreter." It is significant that Yeats was quite willing to write, for an anthology, a comment on one of his poems *so long* as the comment did not appear over his own name. "If an author interprets a poem of his own," he explained to the editor, "he limits its suggestibility." The poet is eager to be understood. But whereas the comments of a critic may raise the curtain on a reader's understanding of a poem, the poet's own comments drop the curtain. We must therefore not mistake the defensive gesture of a poet like Yeats or Eliot for a declaration of his critical theory.

In this paper, accordingly, I wish, not to advance any new proposition, but only to re-assert the accepted critical principle* that for any given poem there

---

*A more philosophical approach to some of the issues treated in this paper is to be found in René Wellek's "The Mode of Existence of a Literary Work of Art," reprinted in Robert Wooster Stallman's *Critiques and Essays in Criticism, 1920-1948* (New York, 1949), pp. 210-223.

are correct and incorrect readings, and to illustrate the process by which the correctness of a reading may be proved or disproved. For logical proof, though not experimental proof, is at least as possible in the interpretation of poetry as it is, say, in a court of law.

Let me illustrate by presenting two problems in interpretation. The first is an untitled poem by Emily Dickinson:

Where ships of purple gently toss
On seas of daffodil,
Fantastic sailors mingle,
And then—the wharf is still.

The second consists of a pair of poems, one by Walt Whitman, the other by Herman Melville. The poem by Whitman (1819-1892) appeared in his volume of Civil War poems, *Drum-Taps*. Melville, who was Whitman's almost exact contemporary (1819-1891), also published a book of war poems (*Battle-Pieces*), though the following poem did not appear in it.

AN ARMY CORPS ON THE MARCH

With its cloud of skirmishers in advance,
With now the sound of a single shot snapping like a whip, and now an irregular volley,
The swarming ranks press on and on, the dense brigades press on,
Glittering dimly, toiling under the sun—the dust-cover'd men,
In columns rise and fall to the undulations of the ground,
With artillery interspers'd—the wheels rumble, the horses sweat,
As the army corps advances.

THE NIGHT-MARCH

With banners furled, and clarions mute,
    An army passes in the night;
And beaming spears and helms salute
    The dark with bright.

In silence deep the legions stream,
    With open ranks, in order true;
Over boundless plains they stream and gleam—
    No chief in view!

Afar, in twinkling distance lost,
    (So legends tell) he lonely wends
And back through all that shining host
    His mandate sends.

I ask you with the Dickinson poem merely to decide what it is about; with the Whitman and Melville poems, to determine the principal difference between them. The criteria used for judging any interpretation of a poem are two: (1) A correct interpretation, if the poem is a successful one, must be able to account satisfactorily for any detail of the poem. If it is contradicted by any detail, it is wrong. Of several interpretations, the best is that which most fully explains the details of the poem without itself being contradicted by any detail. (2) If more than one interpretation satisfactorily accounts for all the details of the poem, the best is that which is most economical, i.e., which relies on the fewest assumptions not grounded in the poem itself. Thomas Huxley illustrates this principle of judgment in a different area in one of his essays. If, he says, on coming downstairs in the morning we find our silverware missing, the window open, the mark of a dirty hand on the window frame, and the impress of a hobnailed boot on the gravel outside, we logically conclude that the silverware has been stolen by a human thief. It *is* possible, of course, that the silverware was taken by a monkey and that a man with dirty hands and hobnailed boots looked in the window afterwards; but this explanation is far less probable, for, though it too accounts for all the facts, it rests on too many additional assumptions. It is, as we would say, too "far-fetched."

These two criteria, I ask you to notice, are not different from those we bring to the judgment of a new scientific hypothesis. Of such we ask (1) that it satisfactorily account for as many as possible of the known facts without being contradicted by any fact, (2) that it be the simplest or most economical of alternative ways of accounting for these facts.

Now let us turn to our poems.

Several years ago I presented the Emily Dickinson poem to a number of students and colleagues and discovered that not one of them interpreted the poem as I did. Almost universally they read the poem as being descriptive of a scene in a garden or meadow. A consensus of their interpretations runs as follows:

Tall purple flowers (iris?) stand above the daffodils and are tossed in the breeze. Bees and butterflies ("fantastic sailors") mingle with the flowers. The wind stops, and then the garden is still.

Beside this let me place the interpretation which I hope to prove the correct one:

The poem is a description of a sunset. The "ships of purple" are clouds. The "seas of daffodil" are skies colored golden by the setting sun. The "fantastic sailors" are the shifting colors of the sunset, like old-fashioned seamen dressed in gorgeous garments of many colors brought from exotic lands. The sun sinks, and the wharf (the earth where the sun set—the scene of this colorful activity) is still.

How do we demonstrate the "sunset" reading to be correct and the "garden" reading to be incorrect? By some such argument as this:
"Ships of purple" is an apter metaphor for clouds than for flowers, as to both size and motion (we often speak of clouds as "sailing"). "Daffodil" would normally be in the plural if it referred to flowers rather than to color: why would not the poet say "On a sea of daffodils"? Also, the grammatical parallel between "of purple" and "of daffodil" suggests a parallelism of meaning. If we interpret "purple" as a color, we are pushed by this parallelism to interpret "daffodil" as a color likewise. "Mingle" fits better the intertwining colors of the sunset than it does the behavior of bees, which mingle with flowers perhaps but not, except in the hive, with each other. The "garden" reading provides no literal meaning for "wharf." The "garden" reading, to explain why the wharf becomes "still," demands the additional assumption that the wind stops (why should it? and would the bees and butterflies stop their activity if it did?); the disappearance of the sun, in contrast, is inevitable and implicit in the sunset image. Finally, the luxuriance of imagination manifested in the poem is the more natural consequence of looking at clouds and sunset sky than at flowers. We look at clouds and see all sorts of things—ships, castles, animals, landscape— but it takes some straining to conjure up a scene such as this one from a garden.

The "garden" reading is therefore incorrect because it fails to account for some details in the poem (the wharf), because it is contradicted by some details (the singular use of "daffodil"), because it explains some details less satisfactorily than the "sunset" reading ("ships of purple," "mingle"), and finally because it rests on assumptions not grounded in the poem itself (the wind stops). The "sunset" reading explains all these details satisfactorily.

The Whitman-Melville problem I once presented as a writing assignment to a college English class. Again I received not a single correct solution. I should confess, however, that I am guilty of having planted a false clue. The false clue lies in the information that Melville wrote a book of poems about the Civil War— perfectly true, of course, but totally irrelevant. This poem is not about the Civil War, as is manifest from "spears and helms"—items not much stocked by Civil War quartermasters. More important, this poem is not about war at all. The main difference between this poem and Whitman's is that Whitman's is literal, Melville's metaphorical. Whitman's is about an army corps on the march; Melville's is about the stars.

My students immediately identified this subject matter when I wrote the Melville poem on the board and circled five words: "beaming," "bright," "gleam," "twinkling," "shining." The five words together form a constellation whose reference, once the pattern is recognized, is almost immediately clear. That "twinkling" modifies "distance" and that "shining" modifies "host" provides additional confirmation. The phrase "host of heaven" is used extensively for stars in the Bible.

Starting from this point, the proof proceeds with logical rigor: (1) The close repetition of "beaming," "bright," "gleam," "twinkling," and "shining" immediately suggests stars. (2) The setting is night. (3) The poem emphasizes the silence of the procession, which moves "in silence deep" and "with clarions mute." (No actual army, of course, no matter how secret its movements, is ever quite so stealthy. In Whitman's poem "the wheels rumble," as indeed wheels do.) (4) The poem also emphasizes the idea of infinite space: the army marches "over boundless plains"; its leader is "Afar, in twinkling distance lost." (5) The army marches "With open ranks, in order true"—a formation more star-like than military. No actual legions ever "stream" in perfect order; but the stars keep an eternally fixed but open relation to each other. (6) Finally, no commander of this army is in view—a situation especially unusual in an army proceeding in perfect order. Indeed, the "army" interpretation cannot explain this detail without assumptions grounded *outside* the poem.

The real difficulty of interpreting the Melville poem comes, of course, at this point, for the Melville poem is not simply descriptive, as Whitman's is, but philosophical. As I read it, the poem poses the question of the existence of God. No God is observable in the heavens (which are silent), yet the stars follow an "order true," and legends (e.g., the Bible) tell us that God orders them. These stories, however, are indeed "legends," i.e., they are of doubtful authenticity; and even if they be true, the God they speak of is "Afar, in twinkling distance lost," not in daily confrontation of man or nature. One hundred years earlier a poet writing on this theme would have declared without hesitation that "The heavens declare the glory of God, the firmament showeth his handiwork"; Melville ends his poem with a question or a doubt. In the nineteenth century the argument from design had been shattered.

If a poem, then, does have a determinable meaning—if, in the interpretation of poetry, we can't say that "anything goes"—why does the opposite theory so often arise? Is it because of some false analogy drawn with music or abstract art? Perhaps. But, first of all, it arises because, within limits, there is truth in it. A poem—in fact, any pattern of words—*defines an area of meaning*, no more. Any interpretation is acceptable *which lies within that area.* The word "horse" may justifiably call up in a reader's mind the image of a black, a roan, or a white horse; a stallion, a mare, or a gelding; even a wooden saw horse, a human "work horse," or a female "clothes horse." But as soon as the word is combined with another, say "roan," the area of meaning is drastically reduced. It can still be stallion, mare, or gelding; but it cannot be a white or black horse, a saw horse, "work horse," or "clothes horse." Further expansions of the context limit the meanings still further. But *even without context* the word cannot mean *cow.*

In poetry, context may function to expand meaning as well as to limit it. Words in poetry thus have richer meanings than in prose—they may exhibit purposeful ambiguities—but the meanings are still confined to a certain area. With a poem like Whitman's that area is fairly narrowly circumscribed. The reader may legitimately see a Northern or a Southern army (if he knows nothing of Whitman's life); in fact, if the poem is removed from its context in *Drum-Taps* he may legitimately see a Revolutionary War army; but in no case may he interpret the poem as being about stars.

The areas of greatest meaning are created by symbolical poems. "A symbol," writes John Ciardi, "is like a rock dropped into a pool: it sends out ripples in all directions, and the ripples are in motion. Who can say where the last ripple disappears?" True. But even a symbol does not have unlimited meaning. The pool in which the rock is dropped has borders. A symbol in literature is made up of words which, by the way they are used, have acquired a sometimes tremendously increased area of meaning. To switch from Ciardi's figure, we may envision such a symbol as a powerful beam of light flashed out into the darkness by a searchlight from a point on earth. The cone of light is the area of meaning. Its point is precise and easily located. But its base fades out into the atmosphere. Its meanings are therefore almost infinite. But they are not unlimited. They must be found, at whatever distance from the apex, within the circumference of the cone.

By the very nature of the case the process of proof or demonstration with symbolic literature is more difficult than with non-symbolic, just as complex logical problems are more difficult than the simple ones by which logicians demonstrate their principles. Scholars will continue to debate the meanings of the "white whale" in *Moby-Dick* for years to come. Their argument, however, has meaning. Some interpretations do make more sense than others. More than one meaning may be valid, but not just *any* meaning can be. The white whale is not an inkblot, not even a white inkblot.

Let me illustrate with a poem by William Blake:

THE SICK ROSE

O Rose, thou art sick!
The invisible worm
That flies in the night,
In the howling storm,

Has found out thy bed
Of crimson joy,
And his dark secret love
Does thy life destroy.

The essential difference between a metaphor and a literary symbol is that a metaphor means something *else* than what it is, a literary symbol means something *more* than what it is. In the words of Robert Penn Warren, a symbol "partakes of the reality which it renders intelligible"; in the words of E. E. Stoll, a symbol "means what it says and another thing besides." If we use I. A. Richards' terms "vehicle" and "tenor" for the two things equated by a metaphor, we must say that with a symbol the vehicle is *part* of the tenor. The vehicle in this case is not like one of those long trucks we see on the highways carrying automobiles from manufacturer to dealer; it is more like a new automobile filled with presents at Christmas time, the automobile being part of the gift. Melville's *Night-March* is not really about an army at all; Blake's poem *is* about a rose and a cankerworm.

But Blake's poem is so richly organized that the rose and the worm refuse to remain a rose and a worm. The phrase "dark secret love" is too strong to be confined to the feeding of the worm on the rose; "thy bed of crimson joy" suggests much more than the rose bed which it literally denotes. The powerful connotations of these phrases, added to those of "sick," "invisible," "night," and "howling storm," and combined with the capitalization of "Rose" and the personification of the flower, force the reader to seek for additional meanings. Almost immediately the Rose suggests a maiden and the worm her secret lover; but these meanings in turn suggest still broader meanings as the cone of light broadens. The poem has been read by different readers as referring to the destruction of joyous physical love by jealousy, deceit, concealment, or the possessive instinct; of innocence by experience; of humanity by Satan; of imagination and joy by analytic reason; of life by death. Some of these meanings are suggested entirely by the poem itself, some by a knowledge also of Blake's other writings.

It is not my purpose here to make a detailed examination of these interpretations in the light of my two criteria. My belief is that a case can be made for *all* of them; that the symbols allow them all; that we are not forced to choose between them, as we *are* forced to choose between the two interpretations of the Dickinson poem or the one by Melville. But *if* the rose can mean love, innocence, humanity, imagination, and life; and *if* the worm can mean the flesh, jealousy, deceit, concealment, possessiveness, experience, Satan, rationalism, death (and more), *can* the two symbols therefore mean just anything? The answer is No. The rose must always represent something beautiful or desirable or good. The worm must always be some kind of corrupting agent. Both symbols define an area of meaning, and a viable interpretation must fall within that area. Blake's poem is not about the elimination of social injustice by an enlightened society; it is not about the eradication of sin by God; it is not about the triumph of freedom over tyranny. Any correct interpretation must satisfactorily explain the details of the poem without being contradicted by any detail; the best interpretations will rely on the fewest assumptions not grounded in the poem itself.

A rose is a rose is a rose, and is more than a rose. But a rose is not an inkblot. Nor is a poem.

Postscript

Ordinarily we have only the internal evidence of the poem itself on which to rest an interpretation. For the Emily Dickinson poem, as I discovered by consulting Thomas H. Johnson's definitive three-volume edition of *The Poems of Emily Dickinson* (Cambridge: Harvard University Press, 1955) some time after the incident related, there is external proof also of the "sunset" reading. The poem (265 in the Johnson edition) was first published in 1891 under the title "Sunset." Though this title was editorially supplied by T. W. Higginson after the poet's death, its correctness is established by two other poems in which she uses substantially the same imagery (yellow and purple, sea and ships). One poem (266) itself contains the word "sunset"; the other (1622) was entitled "Sunset" by the poet in a letter to a friend. Sunset was one of Emily Dickinson's favorite subjects. Johnson's index lists thirty-two poems under this entry. Others using the same color-imagery—purple and yellow (amber, gold) are 219, 228, 716, 1032, and 1650.

After the first publication of this essay, in a periodical, I received letters from several readers arguing for a literal interpretation—one in which the poem is about real ships, real seas, real sailors, and a real wharf. In the words of one correspondent: "Ships are being loaded at a busy wharf in a beautiful and colorful sunset. The ships, tossing gently, appear dark and purplish against the bright sky; the sea is yellow in the sunlight. The sailors, too, are colored by the sunset, and their forms, silhouetted against the sunset sky, appear shadowy, fantastic. Then the ships are loaded; the sailors board the ships. After the ships depart, the wharf is still, no longer bustling with life as night descends." To this interpretation I could raise several objections, one being that the sunset itself now becomes an assumption brought in from outside the poem (to explain the fantastic colors). My chief objection to a literal interpretation, however, is that it makes the poem commonplace—something any versifier could have written. Emily Dickinson's mind seldom worked in such a dull way. Hers was a highly metaphorical imagination, and when she looked at something in nature she characteristically fancied it as something else. The motivating impulse of her descriptive poems was a delighted apprehension of similitude. This is what makes them exciting.

The Importance of Tone
in the Interpretation of Literature

When we speak of *tone* in connection with language, we refer to that element of an utterance which indicates the speaker's or writer's attitude toward his subject, his listener, or himself. In spoken language this feeling or attitude is indicated chiefly by tone of voice. The words "My dear Mary" may be so uttered as to suggest that the speaker is a patient-philosopher-explaining-the-obvious-to-an-idiot-child, or they may be made to express "I love you I love you I love you." In written language these emotional meanings must be expressed by a different means—by the words and images chosen, their arrangement, and their context. The words "My dear Mary" at the beginning of a letter will have their tone defined by what follows (by context), but if the letter begins "My darling Mary" or "Mary, my dear," the tone is more immediately established.

Obviously tone is an important part of meaning. It may even be the most important part of meaning. In communication with pet animals or babies, the tone of voice we use is far more important than the words we use. In interpreting literature the reader who understands the literal content of a poem but who mistakes its tone may be much further from understanding the poem than the reader who makes mistakes about its literal content but who understands the tone. Usually, misinterpretation of one leads to misinterpretation of the other, but understanding one without understanding the other is both hypothetically and actually possible.

My purpose in this essay is to emphasize the importance of tone in interpretation, and to illustrate the techniques by which it is determined. I shall do so by examining three pairs of poems on similar subjects, in each of which one poem is fairly simple in tone, the other more complex.

The first pair consists of two unabashedly didactic poems, each of which draws an "example" from a butterfly:

THE EXAMPLE

Here's an example from
 A Butterfly;
That on a rough, hard rock
 Happy can lie;
Friendless and all alone
On this unsweetened stone.

Now let my bed be hard,
    No care take I;
I'll make my joy like this
    Small Butterfly,
Whose happy heart has power
To make a stone a flower.

W. H. Davies

TWO BUTTERFLIES WENT OUT AT NOON

Two butterflies went out at noon
And waltzed upon a farm,
And then espied circumference
And caught a ride with him;

Then lost themselves and found themselves
In eddies of the sun
Till rapture missed her footing
And both were wrecked in noon.

To all surviving butterflies
Be this biography
Example, and monition
To entomology.*

Emily Dickinson

The first poem is straightforward and direct in its approach both to its subject and to its reader. Its simplicity of language and of form support its meaning. The poem means what it says: Happiness comes from within; the happy heart can make its own joy out of a plain, hard life. The didactic purpose is not tacked on in a moral, but is announced in the first line and informs the whole poem. The candor of this purpose and the simplicity of the poem give it a quiet appeal, a naive charm. In the tone of the poem there are no complications.

In the second poem, however, there is a sharp shift of tone between the first two stanzas and the third. In the first two stanzas the language and the images are fanciful, extravagent, and delightful. The butterflies waltz, they catch a ride with circumference, they play hide and seek in eddying streams of sunlight. They give themselves up to rapture, and they are "wrecked in noon." The tone of these stanzas is particularly set by such words as "waltzed," "sun," and "rapture." The third stanza draws the moral, and does so in heavy, pretentiously pe-

*This poem was left unfinished by its author. The version given here is that published in *Bolts of Melody*, ed. by Mabel Loomis Todd and Millicent Todd Bingham in 1945. The variants from which the editors chose are fully listed in *The Poems of Emily Dickinson*. ed. by Thomas H. Johnson (Cambridge, Mass., 1955), vol. II, p. 410.

dantic language—"biography" for life, "monition" for warning, and "entomology" for insects. How seriously are we to take this "monition"? Is the poet in all earnestness advising us never to give ourselves up to ecstasy lest we come to grief? Or doesn't she rather make the experience described in the first two stanzas more attractive to us than the caution recommended in the third, even though the former does end in disaster? The clue is in the language. For the language of the third stanza is that of a person who has most certainly never waltzed. Its very over-solemnity tells us that the poet herself is not solemn: her long face and her grave tones slyly mock the advice that she is giving. To be sure, she is telling us that if we dance in the rain we may catch our deaths of pneumonia, that the person who gives up his heart completely to joy of any kind—love, for instance—may be "wrecked in noon." But her tone does not endorse the prudent pragmatism of the advice that she seems to be giving. Perhaps to be "wrecked in noon" is preferable to having never known the "eddies of the sun."

My second pair of poems are both written about the moon:

A SONNET OF THE MOON

Look how the pale Queen of the silent night
Doth cause the ocean to attend upon her,
And he, as long as she is in his sight,
With his full tide is ready her to honor;
But when the silver waggon of the Moon
Is mounted up so high he cannot follow,
The sea calls home his crystal waves to moan,
And with low ebb doth manifest his sorrow.

So you, that are the sovereign of my heart,
Have all my joys attending on your will,
My joys low-ebbing when you do depart,
When you return, their tide my heart doth fill.
So as you come and as you do depart,
Joys ebb and flow within my tender heart.

      Charles Best

TARGET

The moon holds nothing in her arms;
    She is as empty as a drum.
She is a cipher, though she charms;
    She is delectable but dumb.
She has no factories or farms,
    Or men to sound the fire-alarms
When the marauding missiles come.

We have no cause to spare that face
    Suspended fatly in the sky.
She does not help the human race.
    Surely, she shines when bats flit by
And burglars seek their burgling-place
    And lovers in a soft embrace
    Among the whispering bushes lie—

But that is all. Dogs still will bark
    When cottage doors are lightly knocked,
And poachers crawl about the park
    Cursing the glint on guns halfcocked;
None of the creatures of the dark
    Will, in their self-absorption, mark
    That visage growing slightly pocked.

                    R. P. Lister

These two poems differ widely in time of composition. The first, published soon after the death of Queen Elizabeth I, reflects in its imagery and thought the panoply of the Renaissance court with its numerous splendid attendants, its strong ethic of loyalty, and its centralization of power in the queen. The second, published during the reign of Elizabeth II, is a space-age poem, taking its occasion from the first missile-shots made at the moon. In subject also the two poems really differ: the first poem is about love, and uses the moon simply as metaphorical vehicle for paying tribute to the beloved. The second poem is about the moon and moon-shots, and uses love to make a point in what it says about the moon. In tone the poems are even more sharply different. The first is straightforward and romantic: it treats the moon in its traditional role as an object of beauty and "queen" of the night-time sky and pays tribute to the beloved by comparing her to the moon in loveliness and power. The tone of the second is sardonic and more complex: we must not decide too quickly what the poem "says."

If we read it without heeding tone, this poem takes a hard-headed and utilitarian attitude. The moon, it says, is lifeless and almost useless, and shooting missiles at it will therefore do no harm. The moon does perform a slight service, to be sure, in that it makes it harder for burglars to commit thefts and for lovers to carry on clandestine affairs. But dogs serve the same purpose and will continue to do so; and the moon itself, though growing slightly pocked, will continue to glint on the halfcocked guns of the burglars. Moreover, none of the night's creatures—dogs, lovers, or burglars—will notice the pocking of the moon. They are all too absorbed in themselves.

The moon is depreciated in value and in romantic appeal throughout the poem. Though personified (referred to as "she" and given "arms" and a "face" or "visage"), the effect of this personification is countered by the fact that she "holds nothing in her arms," is "empty as a drum," is a "cipher," and is "dumb." The comparisons to drum and cipher indicate both roundness and emptiness. There is nothing like the full romantic personification of the moon in Best's poem as a Queen with her attendant court. Rather than being romantically "pale," or traditionally slim, slender, full, or refulgent, this moon is "suspended fatly" in the sky. Fatly, and, the context urges one to add, fatuously.

The value of love, with which the moon is traditionally associated, is also depreciated in the poem. Lovers are put in the same category as burglars. Like burglars, their affairs are stealthy and clandestine. Like burglars, they are dishonest, for, reclining "among the whispering bushes" they whisper romantic lies to each other. Almost the only usefulness the moon has is that it makes their concealment more difficult. And the usefulness of dogs is that they bark both at lovers ("when cottage doors are lightly knocked") and at burglars.

But before drawing conclusions, we should notice that the poet's attitude toward lovers is after all ambiguous. This ambiguity is partly expressed in the word "lie." The first and most obvious meaning of the word is *recline*. But here the word is torn from its natural sentence order and placed at the end of its clause. It is also at the end of a line and, without finishing a sentence, is at the end of a stanza. It bears the additional weight of rhyme. By this combination of rhetorical devices the poet has forced a peculiar emphasis on the word, which makes us consider it more closely, and which finally makes us read it also in the sense of *deceive*. If it is taken in its first sense only, however, these lines say nothing unfavorable to the lovers; and, in fact, despite their juxtaposition to burglars, the lovers are treated rather favorably than otherwise. The connotations of "soft embrace" and "whispering bushes" are favorable and predispose us to take a traditionally romantic attitude toward them. Moreover, lovers are people (and produce more people), and thus the lovers in their "soft embrace" are in contrast to the moon, who "holds nothing in her arms" and is uninhabited.

But the moon, too, is treated ambiguously. True, she is empty and a cipher, people-less and useless; nevertheless, she "charms" and is "delectable." Moreover, the whole second stanza is subtly ambiguous in its attitude toward the moon.

She does not help the human race.
Surely, she shines when bats flit by
And burglars seek their burgling-place
And lovers in a soft embrace
Among the whispering bushes lie—

These lines can be read as meaning that she does after all help the human race by helping to expose burglars and lovers, as we have read them above; or they can be read to mean that she does after all help *part* of the human race, namely, burglars and lovers. She helps the burglars find their burgling-place, and she helps lovers, as the moon has always helped lovers, by furnishing romantic setting and inspiration. The poet has it both ways. And in the second of these ways, if we accept a favorable attitude toward lovers, the moon does a desirable job.

And, in fact, we must finally accept a favorable attitude toward both lovers and moon. For the missiles are "marauding" and they leave the moon "pocked": our attitude is not favorable toward either marauders or pock-marks. Thus the poet, though he pretends to be matter-of-fact and utilitarian and not-to-be-taken-in by romantic illusions about moonlight and love, is, in fact, like Best, the champion of moonlight and love and all that is "delectable" and beautiful. And the tone of the poem, though on the surface cynical, hard-headed, and utilitarian, when read more deeply reveals an ironic protest against the desecration of the moon.*

My third pair of poems are both by one poet, Walter Savage Landor, and both are on the subject of old age. A period of seven years separates them in publication, but both were written when Landor was over seventy.

TO AGE

Welcome, old friend! These many years
  Have we lived door by door;
The Fates have laid aside their shears
  Perhaps for some few more.

I was indocile at an age
  When better boys were taught,
But thou at length hast made me sage,
  If I am sage in aught.

Little I know from other men,
  Too little they from me,
But thou hast pointed well the pen
  That writes these lines to thee.

Thanks for expelling Fear and Hope,
  One vile, the other vain;
One's scourge, the other's telescope,
  I shall not see again.

---

*The reader should notice how the rhymes, all of which contain a "k," make the sounds of barking, knocking, and pocking throughout the last stanza.

Rather what lies before my feet
    My notice shall engage—
He who hath braved Youth's dizzy heat
    Dreads not the frost of Age.

YES; I WRITE VERSES

Yes; I write verses now and then,
But blunt and flaccid is my pen,
No longer talked of by young men
    As rather clever;
In the last quarter are my eyes,
You see it by their form and size;
Is it not time then to be wise?
    Or now or never.

Fairest that ever sprang from Eve!
While Time allows the short reprieve,
Just look at me! would you believe
    'Twas once a lover?
I cannot clear the five-bar gate,
But, trying first its timbers' state,
Climb stiffly up, take breath, and wait
    To trundle over.

Through gallopade I cannot swing
The entangling blooms of Beauty's spring,
I cannot say the tender thing,
    Be't true or false,
And am beginning to opine
Those girls are only half-divine
Whose waists yon wicked boys entwine
    In giddy waltz.

I fear that arm above that shoulder,
I wish them wiser, graver, older,
Sedater, and no harm if colder,
    And panting less.
Ah! people were not half so wild
In former days, when, starchly mild,
Upon her high-heeled Essex smiled
    The brave Queen Bess.

How are we to explain the difference in these two poems, both written by
the same poet? In one he welcomes old age and says that it has brought him wis-

dom and sharpened his pen. In the other he laments old age and says that it has diminished his powers and blunted his pen. Are we to conclude that Landor's attitude sharply changed in the seven years that separated the two poems? This theory would be attractive except that actually the first of the two, as printed above, was the later written, so we cannot explain the change on the supposition of physical and mental decline. Are we to assume then that Landor felt different ways about old age on different days and wrote one poem out of one mood and the other out of a different? Nothing could be more natural or more consistent with the inconsistent facts of human nature. But before we settle on this conclusion, we had best again examine the tone of the two poems.

Again the first of the two poems is the simpler. There is pride in its tone, and also humility; there is gratitude and determination and stoicism. But on the whole the tone is forthright and uncomplicated. It is the second poem which demands close inspection.

First, the situation. The speaker (since he is a poet and was once a lover, we may not unfairly identify him with Landor) is at a ball watching the young people waltz. (The waltz, which had been introduced into England in 1815, was regarded by some of the older generation as a daring and improper dance.) A young lady has come courteously up to the old gentleman and has asked him, "Aren't you Mr. Landor the poet?" or "Don't you write poetry?" or some such. The poem is Landor's reply.

The reply might at first seem the typical querulous grumbling of self-pitying old age. The poet complains of his failing eyesight and his stiffening limbs: he can no longer vault the five-bar gate or join in a sprightly dance. He complains also of mental decline: he can no longer write clever verses, as he once did, or speak the gallant and tender speech—"Be't true or false"—to the opposite sex. Finally, in the characteristic posture of old age, he laments the wildness of the younger generation and expresses a longing for the "good old days" when things were statelier and more fitting than they are today.

But are we to take all this at face value? May not Landor be "playing a game" with the young lady by pretending—or half-pretending (for he doesn't really mean to fool her)—to be the crumbling old monument that she perhaps expected to find? Will she go away from this conversation merely with a sense of having done her duty by making the conscientious inquiry, or will she go away delighted at having discovered a gallant and charming old man? All depends upon his tone; and since we are not there like the young lady to hear the humor in his voice, or to observe the twinkle in his eye, we must *infer* these from his language.

Some people are able to triumph over their pains and misfortunes by converting them into the materials of humor. They steal the sting from their miseries by making them into a comic saga. Of course, no man but regrets the dimming of his eyesight and the stiffening of his limbs, and there is a genuine wistfulness in

Landor's references to his physical decline. Nevertheless, the striking thing about his account of his infirmities is the imaginative humor with which he describes them. Thus, he draws his metaphor for his dimming eyesight from the phases of the moon: "In the last quarter are my eyes." The wit of the comparison undercuts the complaint. Then, turning to the young lady he commands her:

> Just look at me! would you believe
> 'Twas once a lover?

It was once a lover! A suppressed chuckle buoys up his use of the neuter pronoun. And Landor's complaint about his inability to vault the five-bar gate is elaborated into a lovingly-detailed humorous description of his present procedure: First he grasps the bars and shakes them, testing their firmness. Next he climbs stiffly up, pauses at the top to regain his breath and gather strength, then "trundles" over. In the two comma-marked pauses which interrupt and slow down the penultimate line of the description, one almost hears the aged poet puffing for breath. Clearly, here is a man who can laugh at himself. He finds as much humor in the spectacle he presents as might the most detached stander-by.

As for the other infirmities, they are nonexistent. We cannot take seriously his complaint that he "cannot say the tender thing, Be't true or false," when he has just addressed the young lady at his side as "Fairest that ever sprang from Eve!" In fact, we wonder whether, protected by the privilege of age, he may not now flatter the opposite sex even more boldly than when he was younger. At any rate, he has lost none of his gallantry with increasing years and can speak of young ladies as "The entangling blooms of Beauty's spring" as gracefully and as appreciatively as any youthful poet.

Similarly the complaint that his pen is "blunt and flaccid" wilts before the evidence of the completed poem, which is as "clever," as delicious, as neatly put together as anything that Landor composed when younger. The old man still writes well, and knows it.

Once we have established the essential playfulness of Landor's tone, we should be prepared to take at less than face value his remarks about the younger generation and the "good old days" of brave Queen Bess. If indeed the young people go at a pretty fast pace for an old man, and if the poet surprises in himself a half-wish that they would slow down a bit and that the girls would "pant less," he recognizes this wish for what it is and ridicules it by exaggerating it. Rather than being really distressed by the "wickedness" of the boys in putting their arms around the girls' waists publicly, he probably wishes that he might do the same. And if he no longer thinks the girls "divine," he amazingly still thinks of them as "half-divine"—an illusion lost by most men long before they have reached the poet's age of over seventy.

But indeed the old man seems to have held on to a youthful spirit remarkably long:

Is it not time then to be wise?
Or now or never.

The spectacle of a seventy-year-old man resolving to be no longer young and foolish may well excite our admiration, even though (in view of the following line) we may question whether he is fully ready to give up romantic indiscretions even yet. At any rate, let no man lament for Walter Savage Landor or accuse him lightly of self-pity. There's life in the old boy yet!

We have examined three pairs of poems, in each of which the first poem seemed to exhibit a positive attitude toward its subject—the lives of butterflies, the moon and love, old age—and the second poem a negative attitude. On closer examination, however, these differences dissolved, and we found the second poem in the pair also to manifest approval of its subject, though perhaps a more qualified approval than in the first. When a statement means the opposite of what it says, we call it ironical; we must therefore say that the second poem in each of these pairs is ironical. Only in the simplest forms of irony, however, is the meaning confined to the opposite of what is said ("Aren't you a pretty sight!" addressed to the boy who has just fallen into a mud hole). In more complex forms of irony two things are meant at once: both what is said, and the opposite of what is said, though usually there is a stronger emphasis on one side than on the other. Thus Emily Dickinson, if she values rapture over caution, is yet keenly aware of the price that must be paid for it. R. P. Lister, though he approves of both the moon and love, is well aware of the lies romantic lovers tell each other and of the deceptions they perpetrate. And Walter Savage Landor, though he can enjoy his old age, is fully cognizant of its aches and pains and its gradually slackening pace. Moreover, though these three poems are ironical, their irony is not to be located in any specific words or lines; rather it is an irony of the whole, an irony of *tone*. When Landor declares that "blunt and flaccid" is his pen, the words do not strike us with ironic force; it is only later, when we have read the whole, that we realize how they must be qualified. We are brought back, then, to tone as a determining element of meaning. It is tone which tells us what the author feels about his subject, his audience, and himself. But tone is located in no specific element of the poem; it arises from diction, images, figures of speech, structure, even rhymes and meter—in short, from the whole. If we miss any part of this whole, we may miss the tone of the poem. And if we miss its tone, we miss its meaning.

Poetry Begins with Words

The individual poem may begin elsewhere—"with a lump in the throat, a home-sickness or a love-sickness," for Robert Frost; with a feeling in "the pit of the stomach," for A. E. Housman; or even with a tune in the head. But poetry begins with words. The fundamental mark of a poet is not his skill at rhymes or meters, not the nobility of his thoughts or the intensity of his emotions, not even his ability to make images or think in metaphors; it's his way with words. The promising young poet, as W. H. Auden has said, is not the one who wants to write because he has "something important to say," but one who likes "to hang around words and overhear them talking to one another."

Poetry begins with words. All words. The first thing the good poet today learns is that there are no poetic or unpoetic words; there is no special vocabulary from which he must select; the whole province of language lies before him, where to choose. Hamlet's injunction to Horatio, "Absent thee from felicity awhile," is poetry, and so is his statement about Polonius's corpse, "I'll lug the guts into the neighbor room." T. S. Eliot's description of a London church interior, "Inexplicable splendour of Ionian white and gold," is poetry, and so is Robert Frost's "I sha'n't be gone long.—You come too." When Shelley writes, "Life, like a dome of many-coloured glass, / Stains the white radiance of eternity," that's poetry; and when one of Christopher Fry's characters in *The Lady's Not for Burning* calls another, "You slawsy poodle, you tike, / You crapulous puddering pipsqueak!" that's also poetry. A verse-writer errs if he thinks that poetry lies simply in stringing together pretty words into a tinkly tune. *Iridescent, myriad, avatar, glimmering, lucent, amethyst*—it's not collecting words like these and making them go up and down to the dance of meter that constitutes poetry. The beauty of poetry, someone has said, is not the result of putting beautiful words together but of putting words together beautifully. What results from putting beautiful words together is not a poem—which is a balanced set of tensions and countertensions working efficiently together like the muscles in a horse—but something more like a dime-store costume-jewelry counter—lots of glitter and no real value. Poetry can't be made of one word dancing alone, or or a group of words dancing alone; it's always a troupe of words dancing together.

The first necessary equipment for the poet, then, is a knowledge of words. He's got to know their shapes and sizes and colors. He's got to know their past histories, their credit standings, and their habits. Do they hang around on the corners with the drugstore cowboys? Do they work out on the oil rigs with the roughnecks? Do they move only among the Four Hundred in the Social Register? A word's character and personality, like a human being's, is formed by its companions. The poet must know what company they keep.

Take a word like "commit." It means "to do, to perform." But what sort of company does it keep? Bad company. One "commits" a crime, a nuisance, or a folly, or adultery. The word takes color from the company it keeps and gives color to the company it joins. Edward Young in the eighteenth century realized this when he satirized those people who give up their sins and reform their characters from motives of expediency:

> Whoe'er their crimes for interest only quit,
> Sin on in virtue, and good deeds commit.

To say that "commit" turns "good deeds" into "bad deeds" here is to put the case too simply; actually the good deeds become bad deeds and good deeds both at once. A paradox.

Is "commit" a poetic word? One wouldn't have thought so; it sounds more like a legal term. But Young has used it poetically—so that meaning breaks out of it. The poet may use any words so long as he puts them together in the right combinations. Shakespeare used legal terms in his love sonnets, and he made them work. Perhaps the only words generally unavailable for the poet today are those exclusively "poetic": *ere, yon, ope, oft, yore,* and *even* (for *evening*); *o'er, e'er,* and *e'en; dost, lovest,* and *breatheth.* The only words today's poet cannot use are the words no one but he would be tempted to use.

Exactly what did Young do with the word "commit"? He yoked together words which had never been yoked before, and which, once yoked, seemed predestined for each other. And this is what the poet must do. The poet, as T. S. Eliot has said, "dislocates" language into meaning. He puts words together that haven't been put together before. Of course, my students in composition do this also, and the result is chaos. But the poet knows what words, like chemical elements, have valences for each other and will hook on together. He knows what words, like chemical elements, when put together will cause an explosion of meaning. Not an accidental explosion, which is meaningless, but a controlled explosion. When Milton speaks in *Lycidas* of the priests who have entered the church only as a path of worldly advancement, a means of earning their bread, he calls them "blind mouths." Who would have thought of using the words "blind" and "mouths" together? But once Milton has done it, the combination seems inevitable. Wilfred Owen, describing a gas attack on the Western Front in World War I, writes about the fumbling haste of the soldiers to put on their gas masks when the alarm is given:

Gas! GAS! Quick, boys!—An ecstasy of fumbling,
Fitting the clumsy helmets just in time.

"An *ecstasy* of fumbling!" What an unlikely pair, one would have thought. But Owen has joined the two words together in holy matrimony, and the union has been blessed now for more than half a century.

Conversely, the good poet avoids yoking together the words that have been too often put together in the past. Or rather, he resists their powerful natural gravitation toward each other; he jumps up and thrusts them apart when he sees that they are about to embrace in the dull kiss of domestic habit. The *purling brook*, the *whispering breeze, starry eyes* and *ruby lips*, the *proud heart*, the *unfettered soul*: phrases such as these may have had poetic power once, but the meaning has seeped out of them like water from a leaky basin.

Poetry is the most concentrated form of language. It is the art of controlled explosion. The poet, like a gunner, gives his words their explosive power by packing his powder into a confined space, then touching off a spark. More literally, he chooses his words for maximum meaning. Like a man packing a suitcase for a vacation, he leaves out what is unessential and folds small what he needs to take.

An anonymous little poem I'm fond of carries invaluable advice for the poet:

The written word
Should be clean as bone,
Clear as light,
Firm as stone.
Two words are not
As good as one.

I have sometimes presented a bastard version of this to my classes, and asked them to choose the better version:

The spoken or written word
Should be as clean as a bone,
As clear as is the light,
As firm as is a stone.
Two words will never serve
As well as one alone.

Many of them choose wrong. They've been taught to enjoy poetry for its pleasant tinkle rather than for its creation of meaningful experience. But the second version is diluted poetry. Using half again as many words, it says less, because it says it with less impact. Its additional words carry no payload of image, thought, or emotion. They are therefore empty words for the poet.

Poetry is the art of concentration. Marlowe's Faustus asks of Helen of Troy, "Is this the face that launched a thousand ships?" Translated into prose this becomes, "Is this the woman whose face was so beautiful that for her sake a thousand ships were launched?" Twice as many words, and the impact gone. A philosopher might say, "Maturity is the most necessary achievement of man." Shakespeare says, "Ripeness is all."

The poet achieves concentration not only by omitting but by packing. Words, unlike algebraic symbols, are not counters which have only one value and that one value always; words are complexes of meaning, and the poet, unlike the ordinary writer, uses as much of that complex as he can. Every good word consists of three parts: sound, denotation, and connotation. Sound itself, in onomatopoetic words, may be an element of meaning. The denotations of a word, its dictionary-meanings, may be multiple. The connotations, what the word *suggests* above and beyond what it *states*, ray out around the word like the soft halo around the moon.

The multiplicity of denotations possessed by some words is a nuisance to the practical user of language, an embarrassment to the inept poet, and an opportunity for the good one. The poster-maker who, during World War II, put up signs in New York saying "Save Soap and Waste Paper," fell into one kind of trap. John Masefield, making a wish for England in his coronation poem to Elizabeth II, falls into another:

May this old land revive and be
Again a star set in the sea.

In his eagerness to describe England as both a star and a jewel, Masefield forgets that "set" has one meaning used with "jewel" and another with "star": thus his hope for England's revival raises inadvertently a counter-picture of England's being extinguished in everlasting night. Randall Jarrell is more skillful when he writes in a poem, "In Nature there is neither left nor right nor wrong." He makes the word "right" do double duty, getting twice its ordinary value from it.

When a poet uses a word in two denotations, he is making, of course, a pun. But poets have been punsters for serious purposes from way back, and will be as long as the pun conveys two or more meanings at once. Shakespeare's

. . . golden lads and girls all must,
As chimney sweepers, come to dust,

occurs in a funeral dirge. Milton, in a sonnet on his blindness, uses the word "talent" to mean both an aptitude and a Biblical coin; and in *Paradise Lost*, a poem which has never been accused of being humorous, he speaks of an army of pigmies as a "pigmy infantry." In Pope's description of a hunting scene in Windsor Forest,

Oft, as in Airy Rings they skim the Heath,
The clam'rous Plovers feel the Leaden Death,

"Leaden" points literally to the material of which the bullets are made, and metaphorically to the heavy inertness of the death the bullets bring. Sometimes the puns are so unobtrusive that we don't consciously think of them as being puns at all; nevertheless, they are there, quietly doing their work. Keats, addressing the Grecian urn with "Thou still unravished bride of quietness," uses "still" instead of "yet" with a sure poetic instinct.

But connotation is an even richer source of power for the poet. As John Livingston Lowes has pointed out, "The business of words in prose is primarily to *state*; in poetry, not only to state, but also—and sometimes primarily— to *suggest.*" Or as Churchy LaFemme says in *Pogo*, "It ain't so much what a poem says. It's the countless things it don't say . . . all deep!"

Connotations are easiest to see in pairs of words that have the same or almost the same denotation. Thus a "mother" is a female parent, but the word "mother" suggests love, protection, warmth, honor, everything that we pay tribute to on Mother's Day: we have no Female Parent's Day. A "spy" is a secret agent, but "secret agent" suggests mystery, glamour, excitement, and thrilling adventure, while "spy" suggests treachery, meanness, and death by hanging or firing squad. I'd rather be "uninformed" than "ignorant." I like to be told I have an "inquiring mind," but I don't like to be suspected of being "inquisitive." I don't mind too much being told I've behaved "foolishly," but I get angry when I'm told I acted "like a fool." I'd rather be "wealthy" than "rich," intelligent" than "brainy," "famous" than "notorious." The word "breast" in the singular means bosom, and suggests warmth, affection, love, motherhood—everything sacred; add an *s* to the end and it suggests sex and sin, Marilyn Monroe and Mae West. Poe, when he wrote of "the glory that was Greece, and the grandeur that was Rome," made an eternal and memorable distinction between the spiritual achievements of the one civilization and the material achievements of the other. George Santayana also made an important distinction when he wrote, "I . . . love the earth and hate the world." And even Eddie Guest touched on something fundamental when he wrote, "It takes a heap o' livin' in a house t' make it home."

Samuel Butler once pointed out that Coleridge's *The Ancient Mariner* would have lost a good deal of its glamour if it had been called *The Old Sailor*. The word "ancient" has connotations which suggest something worthy of reverence: it implies not only that Coleridge's protagonist is old in years but that he belongs to a past age. The romantic connotations of "mariner" prepare us for a marvelous tale. The connotations of "old sailor" are prosaic and commonplace. And if we call him an "antique salt," the effect is ludicrous. W. S. Gilbert in *The Yarn of the Nancy Bell* calls his main character "an elderly naval man." The comic connotations of this

designation prepare us for the comic nature of Gilbert's narrative. And notice that Gilbert's "elderly naval man" spins a "yarn"; Coleridge's ancient mariner tells a "tale."
Keats's famous lines from the *Ode to a Nightingale* have long served as a touchstone of poetic magic and of romantic fancy. Keats speaks of the song that

> oft-times hath
> Charmed magic casements opening on the foam
> Of perilous seas, in faery lands forlorn.

What a delicate and fragile beauty it is! If we change "casements" to "windows," half the magic is dissipated. Casements *are* windows, but casements are romantic and windows unromantic. Similar damage is done if we try to change "perilous" to "dangerous": "perilous" suggests chivalric adventure and knightly quest, the siege perilous, the castle perilous, and "the light that never was on land or sea." "Dangerous" suggests a red light hanging at a railroad crossing, or a sign saying "Men Working."
But we need not take all our examples from the realm of the romantic. Goldsmith in *The Deserted Village* writes of

> The noisy geese that gabbled o'er the pool,
> The playful children just let loose from school.

Is "just let *loose* from school" the same as "just let *out* from school"? Not quite. The opposite of "out" is "in," but the opposite of "loose" is "bound." Goldsmith knew his schoolchildren and expressed their attitude in his choice of word.
Connotations are not fixed and constant things: like denotations they are controlled by context, and the poet must know how to control them. The slightest changes may make momentous differences. Owen Barfield has pointed out that in Milton's line "Teiresias and Phineus, prophets old," "prophets old" does not mean the same thing as "old prophets." In Milton's phrase the adjective takes on much the same connotations as *ancient* in Coleridge's poem. It suggests a greater venerability and it suggests also an immemorial past—prophets *of* old. Andrew Bradley has pointed out that in two lines from Byron's *Mazeppa*,

> "Bring forth the horse!" the horse was brought:
> In truth he was a noble steed!

the words "horse" and "steed" cannot be interchanged. And notice what happens to the adjective "little" in Samuel Hoffenstein's burlesque *Love Song*:

> Your little hands,
> Your little feet,
> Your little mouth—
> Oh, God, how sweet!

Your little nose,
Your little ears,
Your eyes that shed
Such little tears!

Your little voice
So soft and kind;
Your little soul,
Your little mind!

Mark Twain once wrote that "The difference between the almost-right word and the right word is . . . the difference between the lightning bug and the lightning." Certainly the capacity to use denotations and connotations with precision and power is the fundamental mark of the poet from the humblest to the most exalted. Let me show how connotations and multiple denotations can work together, choosing an illustration from the humblest. Mother Goose rhymes are sometimes awkward, frequently trivial, but sometimes lovely and often memorable. One that remains longest in my memory is the one about the little boy who rode a cock horse to Banbury Cross to see a fine lady upon a white horse. There were no fire engines for boys to ride after then, but in those days of aristocratic splendor and *noblesse oblige*, "a fine lady on a white horse" was something worth seeing:

Ride a cock horse
To Banbury Cross
To see a fine lady upon a white horse.
With rings on her fingers
And bells on her toes,
She shall have music wherever she goes.

Somehow that lady moves always through my memory to music: not only the literal music of bells on her toes, but the metaphorical music of gracious living, courtesy, kindness and beauty. Why? The poet's choice of words is what does it. What happens, for instance, if we substitute for "lady" the word "female," or even "woman"? All the aristocratic fineness and graciousness slip immediately away from her. A woman would not be crossing Banbury Cross on a horse, but on her feet, and a female could only be transported across it in a zoology textbook. And what happens if we take her off her "white" horse and put her on a "black" one? Black horses are as good as white, often better; but centuries of usage have given connotations to "white" of purity and fineness, and opposing connotations to black. More is lost than the relationship of vowel sound between "fine" and "white," though that is lost too. And suppose we take her off her "horse" and put her on an "equine quadruped"? The fact would be the same, but the truth would be destroyed. No lady ever rode on an equine quadruped. If we take the rings off her "fingers" and put them on her "digits," she becomes immediately ludicrous. And what if we take the bells off her "toes" and put them on her "feet"? "Toes" are more fine and delicate than "feet." But the key word in this little rhyme involves not primarily connotation but dual denotation. The fine lady has "rings" on her fingers. "Rings," of course, are jewelry. But put "rings" just before a line containing "bells," and before another line with the word "music," and what happens? A second denotation rings out, and this, aided by the connotations already indicated, transposes the "music" of the last line from the realm of the literal to the metaphorical, and keeps that lady alive in my memory.

Poetry is a multi-dimensional language. It is multi-dimensional in its effects because it touches man along several dimensions of his being—not just, like practical language, along the dimension of his intellectual understanding, but also along the dimensions of his senses, his emotions, and his imagination. And it is multi-dimensional in its effects because it uses multi-dimensional means. It begins with words. From words it moves on to images. On this level, too, it accomplishes maximum ends with a brilliant economy of means. When the lady in Amy Lowell's *Patterns* dreams of provoking her lover to pursuit among her patterned garden paths, she describes him thus:

I should see the sun flashing from his sword-hilt and the buckles on his shoes.
I would choose
To lead him in a maze along the patterned paths,
A bright and laughing maze for my heavy-booted lover
Till he caught me in the shade,
And the buttons of his waistcoat bruised my body as he clasped me,
Aching, melting, unafraid.

Only four points of the lover's appearance and costume are mentioned: his sword-hilt, his buckles, his heavy boots, the buttons on his waistcoat. But these are the four points which most strike her senses: sunlight flashes from the sword-hilt and buckles, the heavy boots thud on the paths, the buttons bruise her bare flesh. The reader's imagination fills in between these salient points, and the resulting picture is more vivid than would be given by the completest of inventories.

From image, poetry moves on to metaphor. Here, too, its tendency is toward the multi-dimensional. When Humbert Wolfe describes the squirrel as sitting "Like a small grey / coffee-pot," the image is brilliant but one-dimensional. But when Stephen Spender writes in one of his poems that "The cripples pass like question marks," the effect is two-dimensional. The question marks not only represent the deformed and hunch-backed shapes of the cripples, they also pose the eternal question of human suffering: *Why?* Similar intensification of meaning takes place in Wilfred Owen's *Mental Cases* when Owen writes of the experience of the shell-shocked veterans in the military hospitals. Their nights are filled with nightmare, and then "The dawn breaks open like a fresh wound." The word "breaks," of course, has one meaning with "dawn" and another with "wound." And the metaphor functions both visually and emotionally. During sunrise, the sun seems to bleed across the sky. Dawn comes to "the mental cases" bringing, not renewed energy and hope, but continued pain and suffering.—One more example. In *The Caged Skylark* the poet-priest Gerard Manley Hopkins writes of the resurrection of the body and the soul. The soul in life is like a caged skylark: it beats against the bars of its body. But the resurrected soul in its resurrected body is like a wild skylark singing in its nest, for the resurrected body is a home, not a prison; it is perfected and ethereal, not an encumbrance.

Man's spirit will be flesh-bound when found at best,
But uncumbered: meadow-down is not distressed
For a rainbow footing it nor he for his bones risen.

What a perfect figure for utter weightlessness! The rainbow supporting its magnificent arch on a meadow bends down not a single blade of grass. Could there anywhere be found an equally effective figure for weightlessness?—Yes, a shadow. But as soon as we make the suggestion, we see the perfect beauty of Hopkins's choice. For a rainbow is not only an image of weightlessness, but a symbol of hope, promise, beauty, joy, everything we associate with the resurrection. A shadow depresses no scales, but it nevertheless depresses the spirit.

Poetry begins with words; it ends with symbols. And symbols send out waves of meaning that dissipate only in outer space.

The Untranslatable Language

Astronomers establish the height of an unknown star through the process of triangulation. By taking bearings on the star from two points a known distance apart, they are able to calculate the distance of the third point, the star. Poetry, however, remains an untriangulated star. Though many bearings have been taken on it, its exact position is still to be determined. Nevertheless, attempts at triangulating it are useful. Though they do not fully identify poetry for us, they tell us helpful things about it.

I shall attempt here to answer one question about poetry by this process of triangulation. The three points of my triangle are three quotations, two of them statements, one a question. Using the statements as fixed points, I shall try to locate an answer to the question.

Here are the three quotations, with the question in the middle: (1) "Poetry provides the one permissible way of saying one thing and meaning another." (2) "If that's what the poet means, why didn't he come right out and say so?" (3) "Poetry is a language that tells us, through a more or less emotional reaction, something that cannot be said."

The first of these quotations comes from an essay by Robert Frost. The second can be ascribed to thousands of students. The third was the response of Edwin Arlington Robinson when asked for a definition of poetry. What is the connection between them?

The statement by Robert Frost frankly admits to the grounds of the student's implied accusation: the poet often does mean something different from what he says: he doesn't "come right out and say" what he means. But whereas Frost thinks it "permissible" and even right for the poet to do this, the student feels that the poet is willfully perverse, that he is engaging in deliberate obfuscation for the pleasure of plaguing schoolchildren, and that perhaps all poetry is a gigantic hoax perpetrated by the poet on a gullible public. The definition by Edwin Arlington Robinson, however, provides an answer to the student's question. The poet says one thing and means another because what he means cannot otherwise be said. This is a hard saying. But in it lies the whole purport and justification of poetry.

What Robert Frost was talking about is the use in poetry of figurative language. The best short definition of figurative language is "language that says one thing and means another." Edwin Arlington Robinson, on the other hand, was talking about poetry itself. This distinction needs to be clear. Not all poetry is figurative. The poet doesn't always say one thing and mean something else. In scores of excellent poems, including some by Robert Frost, there is not a single figure of speech. The poet, like any good magician, has numerous tricks by which he produces that "illusion on the imagination" which, according to Macaulay, constitutes poetry. Sometimes he works his spell with incantatory rhythms, sometimes with repetitive and evocative sounds, sometimes with powerfully connotative words, sometimes with a neatly balanced structure of parallelisms and contrasts—sometimes with figurative language. Poetry has many kinds of magic wands, and figurative language is not equivalent to poetry or even indispensable to it.

Nevertheless, without figurative language, though poems would still exist, poetry would be impoverished. Edwin Arlington Robinson had to resort to figurative language even to define poetry. "Poetry is a language that tells us . . . something that cannot be said." Is not this statement a logical contradiction? Yes; it is the kind of contradiction we know as paradox, one which states what is perceived as a truth. To resolve the paradox—that is, to reduce it to literal language—we should have to say: "Poetry is a language that tells us, through a more or less emotional reaction, something that can be said *in no other way*." But if this is what Robinson meant, why didn't he come right out and say it? Simply because it *doesn't* say all that Robinson meant. For poetry is, after all, a kind of miracle, a wild impossibility; and the literal statement leaves out this wild impossibility, does not tell us what poetry *is*, but only something *about* it.

It is not surprising that a poet should employ figurative language in order to define poetry. What is surprising, and significant, is that the student uses the same evasive tactics of which he accuses the poet. "I'll die if I don't pass this test," he says; but he doesn't notify the undertaker. "I've got two strikes against me already," he declares, without a baseball bat in his hand. "My idea went over like a lead balloon," he proclaims; but he's never seen a lead balloon, and wouldn't mistake it for an idea if he did. Why do even the most unpoetical among us constantly resort to saying one thing and meaning another? Precisely for the reason that the poet does: he can say what he means in no other way. For the student who says "I'll die if I don't pass this test" means something more than that he'll be severely disappointed. What he is really trying to express is not so much a fact as a feeling. "I'll be severely disappointed" expresses the fact, but doesn't express the feeling. It *doesn't* say what he means.

And this brings us to a central truth about poetry. Poetry is not a language for stating facts, for presenting arguments, or for setting forth ideas. The business of poetry is not to state propositions, but to communicate experience. At the center of every poem is a perceiving and feeling human being, real or imagined, explicit or implicit, telling us what the world is like *to him* and therefore what it may be like *to us*. If poetry does often express facts, arguments or ideas, it does so incidentally. Only when these are made part of a human experience vividly communicated, only when they are, as Wordsworth said, "carried alive into the heart by passion," do they become poetry. Poetry is the language of man experiencing.

But now, a difficulty. Human beings are unlimited in their capacity for experience. Languages are limited in their vocabulary for expressing experience. Every human experience is unique. The variety and extent of human experience is infinite. Yet for expressing this infinite variety, the English language has hardly more than 600,000 words. Clearly there is not a word for every human experience, or even for most human experiences. Words come into existence only when they point to a generalized human experience, never when they point to unique human experience.

Languages differ, of course. It is said that the Eskimo language has over fifty words for snow. There is one word for "snow in the air," another for "drifting snow," another for "snow lying on the ground," another for "snow drifed into the house." There are different words for different kinds of snow: for "hard-packed snow," for "soft, watery snow," for "newly-fallen snow," etc. In English we have only three words, snow, sleet, slush. How, thus handicapped, can we begin to express snow's "infinite variety"? Even with a full battery of adjectives and modifying phrases, to put before and after, we shall hardly do the trick, and especially if we wish to render it in terms of experience. For this purpose we must resort to figurative language—to saying one thing and meaning another. We will talk, like Emerson, of "the frolic architecture of the snow." We will say, like Wordsworth describing the wanderings of Lucy Gray,

> With many a wanton stroke
> Her feet disperse the powdery snow
> That rises up like smoke.

If we wish to invite someone for a walk through soft, white, newly-fallen and falling snow in still winter weather we shall do it as Elinor Wylie does it in *Velvet Shoes*:

> Let us walk in the white snow
>   In a soundless space;
> With footsteps quiet and slow,
>   At a tranquil pace,
>   Under veils of white lace.
>
> I shall go shod in silk
>   And you in wool,
> White as white cow's milk,

More beautiful
Than the breast of a gull.
We shall walk through the still town
In a windless peace;
We shall step upon white down,
Upon silver fleece,
Upon softer than these.

We shall walk in velvet shoes:
Wherever we go
Silence will fall like dews
On white silence below.
We shall walk in the snow.

Or if we wish to describe a quite different kind of snow, we may do it as Robert Frost does it in *A Patch of Old Snow*:

There's a patch of old snow in a corner,
That I should have guessed
Was a blow-away paper the rain
Had brought to rest.

It is speckled with grime as if
Small print overspread it,
The news of a day I've forgotten—
If I ever read it.

So necessary is metaphor to the formulation of human experience that a large part of our language has its origins in it. Consider the names we give to flowers. An "aster" is a star, though it is not included in astronomers' charts. "Dandelion" comes from the French phrase "dent de lion," or lion's tooth, though the flower provides employment for neither veterinarian nor dentist. "Daisy" is a double metaphor; it is named for its resemblance to the sun, which in turn is called the eye of the day, or "day's eye." These three names, for most people, have lost their metaphorical force and become merely literal. But dozens of flower names, in varying degrees, retain their metaphorical life. Think of snapdragon, buttercup, bluebonnet, bloodroot, fireweed, goldenrod, cattail, baby's breath, bridal wreath, lady's slipper, bachelor button, Queen Anne's lace, Indian paintbrush, black-eyed Susan, Jack-in-the-pulpit.

But flowers and snow belong to the outer world. If we are limited by our poverty of vocabulary for describing our experience of the outer world (just three words for snow), think how helpless we are when it comes to expressing inner experience. Linguists believe that *all* the words we have for naming emotions originated as metaphors. How else could primitive man talk about what he felt? If he needed a word for tree he could point to one and say "tree," and a connection was henceforth established. But what could he point to for anger, sorrow, or joy? The word "emotion" itself originates in a metaphor: it compares a feeling to a movement—a "motion outward" from the psyche. So also with words for specific emotions. "Astonishment" is being struck by thunder. "Rapture" is being snatched up. "Transport" is being carried away. "Dejection" is being thrown down. "Enthrallment" is being made a thrall or slave. "Aversion" is a turning away. "Disgust" is a bad taste in the mouth. "Anguish" is being caught in a narrow place. "Contentment" is being held together or contained. "Remorse" is being bit again—and again and again. "Chagrin," from a Turkish word, is the rump of a horse, or rough hide, something that rubs you the wrong way. Trace any word that names an emotion and you find its roots in metaphor.

But these metaphors are now dead, and the fossil shells that they have left behind are woefully inadequate for expressing the richness of our inner experience. Even if they were alive, there would not be enough of them. Think of the variety and range of human experience for which we depend on the one word "love." Love may refer to divine love—the love of God for man or of man for God; to mother love; to brotherly love; to the romantic sexual passion of Tristram for Isolt, or to the steady married affection of Darby and Joan; to the puppy love of adolescence; and to the animal experience in a rented motel room of two strangers with each other. By extension the word may even refer to the enthusiasm of a hobbyist for his hobby, or to the greed of a miser for his gold. And each of these kinds of love has infinite shadings and degrees of intensity. Yet for all of them we use the one word "love." How can we do it and even begin to express our experience with any exactitude? Invariably we turn to figurative language, to saying one thing and meaning another.

Since I have quoted Edwin Arlington Robinson and referred to Tristram and Isolt, let me illustrate from Robinson's treatment of that story. In the legend from which he drew, the noble knight Sir Tristram was sent to Ireland by his uncle, King Mark of Cornwall, to fetch Isolt, daughter of the Irish king, back to Cornwall to be King Mark's bride. On the homeward journey Tristram and Isolt conceived a deathless passion for each other, one which made as nothing the subsequent marriage of Isolt and Mark. Because of this passion Tristram was banished for life from Cornwall by his uncle. He went to Brittany, where he met, and married, another Isolt, Isolt of the White Hands, daughter of the King of Brittany. This situation Robinson had to render real for modern readers. How was he to explain how Tristram, passionately and immortally in love with Isolt of Ireland, should marry Isolt of Brittany? How was he to distinguish between Tristram's love for the two Isolts? Having first explained that Isolt of Brittany had loved Tristram ever since his short visit to her father, a year earlier, when she was still a budding girl, Robinson tells us that Tristram, in battle, put her father's foes to flight, and then

> that night,
> Having espied Isolt's forgotten harp,
> He plucked and sang the shadow of himself,
> To her his only self, unwittingly
> Into the soul and fabric of her life,
> Till death should find it there. So day by day
> He fostered in his heart a tenderness
> Unrecognized for more than a kind of fear
> For what imaginable small white pawn
> Her candor and her flame-white loveliness
> Could yet become for the cold game of kings . . .
> Once by the shore
> They lingered while a summer sun went down
> Beyond the shining sea; and it was then
> That sorrow's witchcraft, long at work in him,
> Made pity out of sorrow, and of pity
> Made the pale wine of love that is not love,
> Yet steals from love a name.

In the last five lines of that passage, perfectly and precisely defined, is the expression of a feeling for which the language has no name, or none but "love." Compounded of tenderness, sorrow, and pity, it is yet something more than the sum of these, yet how much less than Tristram's passion for Isolt of Ireland! And how does Robinson achieve this miracle of definition? By an almost magical use of figurative language—by saying one thing and meaning another. There is first the metaphor of sorrow's "witchcraft," converting sorrow into pity and pity into love. This is followed by a second metaphor, "the pale wine of love," in which the perfectly chosen adjective "pale" both identifies a kind of wine and suggests the difference between this love and Tristram's passion for Isolt of Ireland. Then there is the paradox of "love that is not love," followed by the muted personification in "yet steals from love a name." Two metaphors, a paradox, and a personification coalesce to define the otherwise indefinable.

To define a different quality of love, "the marriage of true minds," Shakespeare, in Sonnet 116, likewise uses paradox, metaphor, and personification.

> Let me not to the marriage of true minds
> Admit impediment. Love is not love
> Which alters when it alteration finds,
> Or bends with the remover to remove.
> O no! it is an ever-fixèd mark

That looks on tempests and is never shaken;
It is the star to every wandering bark,
Whose worth's unknown, although his height be taken.

"Love is not love which alters . . . " says Shakespeare. The paradox isolates one sort of attachment from all other sorts, for which we have only the same name. With the metaphor of the star—the "ever-fixèd mark"—the definition is given body and shape: this love is unswerving, lofty, a guide that gives life meaning and direction. The connotations of the star-image are almost endless.

How different is this "never shaken" love from another kind described by Shakespeare in *Two Gentlement of Verona*: early love—unsure yet as to whether it is fully returned, rising to the pinnacles of hope one moment, cast down into the depths of despair the next. To define it, Shakespeare uses metaphor and simile:

Oh, how this Spring of love resembleth
    The uncertain glory of an April day,
Which now shows all the beauty of the sun,
    And by and by a cloud takes all away.

How brilliantly are the metaphor and the simile related! The metaphor, "this Spring of love," would be merely conventional by itself, but by tying it specifically through simile to "The uncertain glory of an April day," Shakespeare gives it resonance, beauty, and exact definition.

Next, let us turn to a different sector in the spectrum of meanings covered by this much-abused word. George Meredith's disillusioned protagonist in *Modern Love*, Section 29, speaks of a purely physical and sensual pleasure no longer sustained and filled by spiritual fervor. Though emotionally revolted by such pleasure, he nevertheless, cynically and despairingly, accepts it.

A kiss is but a kiss now! and no wave
Of a great flood that whirls me to the sea.
But, as you will! we'll sit contentedly,
And eat our pot of honey on the grave.

Because the ecstatic turbulence of the metaphorical series "wave," "flood," "whirls," and "sea" is tamely followed by the passiveness of the verb "sit," a terrible irony informs the adverb "contentedly," suggesting a resignation profoundly *dis*content. Following this, the metaphorical pot of honey, eaten on the brink of the grave, becomes sticky-sweet and horrible. Thus, with the smiling word "contentedly" and the sweet word "honey," Meredith dissects the anatomy of despair. The image makes the flesh creep, as it was designed to do.

One more illustration. The speaker in John Boyle O'Reilly's *A White Rose* seeks to define exactly the quality of his love for a young lady. He does so by distinguishing it from two other kinds of love on either side of it: that is, by indicating its position between two extremes. This is a logical procedure, and O'Reilly is so far merely following the method of a logician who defines his topic by classification and subdivision. But one cannot convey feeling-tone by pure logic. O'Reilly is forced into the use of metaphor, personification, and symbol for defining all three kinds of love he is distinguishing:

A WHITE ROSE

The red rose whispers of passion
And the white rose breathes of love;
Oh, the red rose is a falcon,
And the white rose is a dove.

But I send you a cream-white rosebud,
With a flush on its petal tips;
For the love that is purest and sweetest
Has a kiss of desire on the lips.

At one extreme, physical passion, an almost cruel desire, is identified by the symbol of the red rose, personified as whispering, and metaphorically represented by a falcon. At the other extreme, innocent affection is symbolized by the white rose, personified as breathing, and metaphorically represented as a dove. All that "white" suggests of innocence and purity, all that "rose" suggests of beauty, all that "breathes" suggests of gentleness, and all that "dove" suggests of mildness and peace, combine in this latter definition. But the speaker defines his own love with the symbol of the cream-white rosebud with a "flush" on its petal tips. Notice how perfectly the word "flush" is chosen; it cannot be replaced by "red" or "pink," for it suggests a symbolical delicacy of coloring that these more definite words would destroy. And notice how effectively the rosebud contrasts with the opened roses which precede it: this is a love just beginning to unfold, with the full splendor of its bloom still before it. The comparison of the flush on the petal tips to "a kiss of desire on the lips" completes the definition, which we cannot state in literal language. In a prose paraphrase the connotations of word and symbol, delicate like the flush on the petal tips, vanish; three quarters of the meaning and all of the value simply disappear.

And this ultimately is the distinguishing secret of poetry, its uniqueness as a form of expression. Poetry is the language that cannot be translated. The language of science, the language of mathematics, the language of business, the language of workaday prose: each of these can be translated into other forms without losing any of its usable meaning. But poetry communicates what cannot be said in any words but its own. Without poetry whole areas of human experience would simply have to go unexpressed. Without poetry man is dumb and inarticulate to half his life. Without poetry he can only stammer and stutter in seeking to express what lies deepest in his heart or courses most thrillingly along the channels of his blood.

This point, alas, is not grasped by the student who asks, "If that's what the poet meant, why didn't he come right out and say so?" And the pathos behind that question is that its asker still hasn't truly understood what the poet meant. He has reached the intellectual understanding without having ever put his finger on the true pulse of the poem.

Let us make one more attempt to answer his question, and let us use for the purpose a poem which will not tempt him to ask it—that is, one which intellectually he should have no trouble in understanding. Here is Sara Teasdale's poem *The Net*:

> I made you many and many a song
>   Yet never one told all you are—
> It was as though a net of words
>   Were flung to catch a star;
>
> It was as though I curved my hand
>   And dipped sea-water eagerly,
> Only to find it lost the blue
>   Dark splendor of the sea.

Here, surely, is a poem not difficult to understand, though it expresses itself by saying one thing and meaning another. The simile of flinging out a net of words—that is, no net at all—to catch a star—beautifully symbolizes a futile enterprise. At the same time the net is a metaphor for a song or poem, and the star a symbol for the shining luminosity of the beloved's personality. The simile of dipping sea-water bespeaks the same futile enterprise, and the simile again contains a symbol within it. The dark blue splendor of the sea complements the luminosity of the star. But *why* did the poet use these interlocking complexities of metaphor, simile, and symbol? Why didn't she come right out and say what she meant? For, reduced to the prose paraphrase of thematic statement, what the poet "meant" can be expressed very simply:—"Words cannot say how wonderful you are." Why didn't the poet simply say this, and leave the matter there? If she had, who would have listened? Even her sweetheart would hardly have believed her, and her readers would have turned away with a sigh. For the fact is—and here is a paradox—Sara Teasdale's *poem* actually does catch the star, it does express, or suggest, the inexpressible splendor of her beloved. Its cunningly contrived net of similes and symbols succeeds where prose paraphrase fails. By doing what it says words cannot do, the poem magnificently refutes its own thesis. By saying one thing and meaning another, it "tells us, through a more or less emotional reaction, something that cannot be said."

Four Forms of Metaphor

1

For the poet, declared Aristotle, "the greatest thing by far is to have command of metaphor." For the poetry reader, I would add, the ability to interpret metaphor is equally important. Indeed, the shores of poetry explication are littered with the bones of ships commanded by captains, both amateur and professional, who could not distinguish literal statement from metaphorical, or who, if they could, could not tell what was being compared to what, or why. In this essay I wish to propose not a guaranteed remedy against disaster but a new way of looking at and classifying metaphors, which I think may be useful.

A metaphor, as I define it, consists of a comparison between essentially unlike things. There are two components in every metaphor: the concept being actually discussed, and the thing to which it is compared. I shall refer to these, ordinarily, as the literal term and the figurative term.* The two terms together compose the metaphor.

The established method of classifying metaphors is through grammatical analysis, which begins by identifying the part of speech of the figurative term. According to this system, there are noun metaphors of various kinds; there are also verb metaphors, adjective metaphors, and occasionally adverb and even preposition metaphors. My own analysis will take a different approach. Based on the underlying assumption that both the literal and figurative terms of a metaphor are expressible as substantives, it will classify metaphors according to whether these terms are respectively stated or implied.

Consider, for example, the following passage from *The Life of Samuel Johnson:*

> When I called upon Dr. Johnson next morning, I found him highly satisfied with his colloquial prowess the preceding evening. "Well, (said he,) we had good talk." *Boswell.* "Yes, Sir, you tossed and gored several persons."

A grammatical analysis would classify Boswell's remark as a verb metaphor. The figurative term is "tossed and gored." The literal meaning is something like "humiliated by besting in argument." But actually the literal term of this metaphor is hard to express by this method without using other figurative expressions ("put down," "injured," "treated roughly"). In addition, this analysis omits to mention the image which jumps immediately into the reader's head. Boswell's

---

*I.A. Richards has proposed the terms "tenor" and "vehicle."

metaphor is more easily and naturally described as one in which the literal term (stated) is Dr. Johnson, and the figurative term (implied) is a bull.

Under the assumption that in all metaphors the concepts likened to each other are expressible as substantives, there are four possible forms of metaphor. In the first, both the literal and figurative terms are named; in the second, only the literal term is named; in the third, only the figurative term is named; in the fourth, neither the literal nor the figurative term is named.

2

In Form 1 metaphors both the literal and figurative terms are named. The most familiar type is a simple statement of identity following the formula "*A* is *B*":

> All the world's a stage,
> And all the men and women merely players.
>
> Shakespeare: *As You Like It*

So frequently, in fact, do textbooks use the "*A* is *B*" metaphor as an example that beginning students may be left thinking that all metaphors are of this type. Actually, even Form 1 metaphors exhibit much greater variety. In a very common type, the figurative and literal terms are linked through a genitive construction

> The Bird of Time has but a little way
> To flutter—and the Bird is on the Wing.
>
> FitzGerald: *The Rubaiyat*

They may also be linked by apposition:

> Come into the garden, Maud,
> For the black bat, night, has flown.
>
> Tennyson: *Maud*

Or through the vocative:

> O wild West Wind, thou breath of Autumn's being.
>
> Shelley: *Ode to the West Wind*

Or by means of a demonstrative adjective:

> Be watchful of your beauty, Lady dear!
> How much hangs on that lamp, you cannot tell.
>
> Meredith: *Modern Love*

A transitive verb may be used to "transform" the literal term into the figurative:

> Too long a sacrifice
> Can make a stone of the heart
>
> Yeats: *Easter 1916*

Occasionally the connection may be indicated merely by parallel construction:

> Fools change in England, and new fools arise;
> For, though the immortal species never dies,
> Yet every year new maggots make new flies.
>
> Dryden: Epilogue to "The Husband His Own Cuckold"

The identification can be made through context alone:

> They called me to the window, for
> 'Twas sunset, someone said.
> I only saw an amber farm
> And just a single herd
>
> Of opal cattle feeding far
> Upon so vain a hill
> As even while I looked dissolved . . .
>
> Emily Dickinson

These examples only partially suggest the considerable variety of shapes that Form 1 metaphors may take.*

3

In Form 2 metaphors, only the literal term is named; the figurative term must be inferred. Like Form 1 metaphors, they may take a variety of grammatical shapes. Frequently the metaphorical agent is a verb:

> Tom showed such . . . open-mouthed interest in his narrations that the old guard rubbed up his memory, and launched out into a graphic history of all the performances of the boys on the roads for the last twenty years.
>
> Thomas Hughes: Tom Brown's Schooldays

In this example the verb "rubbed up" transforms memory into a graven brass plate, tarnished, but capable of being shined.

> Sheathe thy impatience; throw cold water on thy choler.
>
> Shakespeare: Merry Wives of Windsor

In the first of these two metaphors, the verb "sheathe" makes impatience into a sword; in the second, the verb plus its object—"throws cold water"—makes choler into a fire. In all three of these examples, the action of the verb is forward, affecting later elements in the sentence. In the example cited from Boswell, the action is backward: the verbs "tossed and gored" work upon their subject,

---

*A thorough grammatical study of metaphor is made by Christine Brooke-Rose in *A Grammar of Metaphor* (London: Secker, 1958). I am partially indebted to her in this analysis.

changing Dr. Johnson into a bull. The action may go in both directions: insofar as "launched" in the Hughes example is not a dead metaphor, it transforms the old guard into a ship and graphic history into a sea.

Though verbs are the most frequent metaphorical agents in Form 2 metaphors, the work can also be done by other parts of speech. In Homer's famous "rosy-fingered dawn" an adjective transforms the dawn into a person. In the following example, two adjectives turn light into an animal, probably a horse:

Pride, like that of the morn,
When the headlong light is loose.

Yeats: The Tower

Occasionally the work will be done by an adverb:

Ye quenchless stars! so eloquently bright.

Robert Montgomery: The Starry Heavens

Here "eloquently" makes the stars into persons. In the next example a noun does the principal work, assisted by the verb:

For we are old, and in our quick'st degrees
The inaudible and noiseless foot of Time
Steals ere we can effect them.

Shakespeare: All's Well That Ends Well

At first glance this metaphor has the appearance of the Form 1 example from *The Rubaiyat* about the "Bird of Time"; actually it is quite different. The noun "foot," though figurative, not literal, is not the figurative term of the metaphor; rather, it is the agent which serves to personify Time. It has no literal equivalent.

Most frequently, in Form 2 metaphors, the work is done by a combination of grammatical elements:

The tawny-hided desert crouches watching her.

Francis Thompson: Sister Songs

In this example the adjective "tawny-hided" and the verb "crouches," plus the participle "watching," make the desert a lion. Neither the verb nor adjective by itself would turn the trick. "Crouches" by itself might point to a tiger; "tawny-hided" by itself could point to a camel.

As may have become apparent, personifications are frequently Form 2 metaphors:

Grim-visaged war hath smoothed his wrinkled front.

Shakespeare: Richard III

4

In form 3 metaphors, only the figurative term is named; the literal term must be inferred. At first thought, the interpretive problem with Form 3 metaphors might seem similar to that with Form 2: one half of the comparison is given: the other half must be guessed. Form 3 metaphors, however, frequently introduce an additional problem: they can easily be mistaken for literal statements.

Night's candles are burnt out.

Shakespeare: Romeo and Juliet

A Form 2 version of this comparison might read "The stars had burnt down to their smoky wicks and flickered out." Here a discrepancy between the logical meanings of the subject and the predicate of the sentence signals the presence of metaphor. In Shakespeare's line, however, the subject and predicate belong to the same area of discourse, and there is no internal clue that Romeo is not talking about real candles—candles that have been burning all night and now, with the approach of morning, have burnt out. We must depend upon a larger context for the clues that indicate a metaphorical reading. When we restore the statement to the speech in which it occurs, we see that Romeo is looking at the sky:

Look love, what envious streaks
Do lace the severing clouds in yonder East—
Night's candles are burnt out and jocund Day
Stands tiptoe on the misty mountain tops.

Because in Form 3 metaphors the writer's real subject of discourse is suppressed, riddles often take this form:

In Spring I look gay
Decked in comely array,
In Summer more clothing I wear;
When colder it grows,
I fling off my clothes,
And in Winter quite naked appear.

Nursery Rhyme

Unless presented in a context which makes us understand we are to guess the answer, this little rhyme might be taken as a perfectly literal bit of nonsense verse. Though the speaker's behavior is eccentric, it is no more so than that of many persons in Edward Lear's limericks. Ordinarily, however, a poem like this one will be printed on a page labeled "Riddles" or followed by the question "Who am I?"

Many proverbs and familiar sayings also are Form 3 metaphors: "You can lead a horse to water, but you can't make him drink," "Don't put the cart before the horse," "Make hay while the sun shines," "There's lots of good fish in the sea," "A rolling stone gathers no moss," "A bird in the hand is worth two in the bush." All these examples show the ambiguous nature of Form 3 metaphors, for all would be literal statements in the appropriate context. A sea captain, taking refuge from a hurricane in the harbor of an unfriendly city, would be speaking literally if he exclaimed, "Any port in a storm!" A respectable lady, seeking shelter from a heavy rain in a low tavern, would be speaking partly metaphorically and partly literally if she made the same exclamation. If she went into the tavern to avoid meeting her ex-husband, she would be speaking pure metaphor.

Allegories also often belong to this class, though often too, as in *Pilgrim's Progress* and *Everyman*, the literal meanings are provided in the names of characters or places. When the meanings are provided, the allegory is an extended Form 1 metaphor. When they are not, it belongs to Form 3. Some allegories go back and forth between the two forms, labeling some characters and places with their intended meanings, but not others.

Extended Form 3 metaphors are not necessarily riddles and allegories, however, and some of the most interesting examples are those in which this kind of metaphor is sustained throughout a poem. A few examples are Frost's *A Hillside Thaw*, Dickinson's *She Sweeps with Many-colored Brooms*, Melville's *The Night-March* and *The Swamp Angel*, Joyce's *I Hear an Army Charging upon the Land*. I shall return later in this essay to the problems of interpretation offered by such poems. For the present let the following short example stand as representative of the class:

> The largest fire ever known
> Occurs each afternoon,
> Discovered is without surprise,
> Proceeds without concern:
> Consumes, and no report to men,
> An Occidental town,
> Rebuilt another morning
> To be again burned down.
>
> · Emily Dickinson

5

In Form 4 metaphors, neither the literal nor the figurative term is named; both must be inferred. I shall not pretend that I have a long list of examples. There are, however, at least four circumstances in which a Form 4 metaphor may occur.

First, both the literal and figurative terms may be represented by parts of speech other than substantives:

> Let us eat and drink, for tomorrow we shall die.
>
> Isaiah 22:13

The literal element in this metaphor is expressed by the verb "shall die" and the figurative element by the adverb "tomorrow." The suppressed literal term is a lifetime and its figurative equivalent is one day. The general meaning is that life is very short.

Second, the apparent subject of the metaphor may be actually the figurative term in some other figure of speech:

> Now all the truth is out,
> Be secret and take defeat
> From any brazen throat.

> Yeats: *To a Friend Whose Work Has Come to Nothing*

The apparent subject in these lines is "throat," but "throat" is a synechdoche for a person. The literal meaning, therefore, is a person or an enemy. The figurative term is an object made of brass, probably a bell or a cannon, for both of these are connected with victory, by either announcing it or aiding in its achievement, and both have "throats."

Third, an extended series of subsidiary metaphors may imply a controlling metaphor of which they all are part:

> All the world's a stage,
> And all the men and women merely players.
> They have their exits and their entrances,
> And one man in his time plays many parts,
> His acts being seven ages. . . .

Jaques' famous speech is a series of related Form 1 and Form 3 metaphors. The world is a stage, men and women are actors, births are entrances, deaths are exits, the different phases of a man's personality development and interest are parts, and the seven ages into which his life may be divided are acts. But these separate metaphors add up, like any column of figures, and imply a total. Their sum is a Form 4 metaphor in which the literal term is life and the figurative term a play.

Fourth, the literal term may be expressed by a pronoun of which the antecedent is left unspecified:

> I like to see it lap the miles,
> And lick the valleys up,
> And stop to feed itself at tanks;
> And then, prodigious, step

> Around a pile of mountains,
> And, supercilious, peer
> In shanties by the sides of roads;
> And then a quarry pare

To fit its sides, and crawl between,
Complaining all the while
In horrid, hooting stanza;
Then chase itself down hill

And neigh like Boanerges;
Then, punctual as a star,
Stop—docile and omnipotent—
At its own stable door.

Emily Dickinson's poem compares a train to a horse. Neither the train nor horse is named. The literal term is represented by an unidentified "it."

6

For the most part I have so far used fairly simple examples, in order to isolate the features I have been discussing. Metaphorical language, however, is often far from simple. Poets typically weave together literal and metaphorical language, the different forms of metaphor, metaphor and other figures of speech. I should like to examine some of these more complicated examples, but first I must introduce two technical terms.

The *extension* of a metaphor may be measured in either of two ways: (1) by the number of words or lines required for its completion, (2) by the number of subsidiary metaphors evolved in its development. By the first of these criteria, Herrick's *To Dianeme* might be called an extended metaphor, but not by the second:

Give me one kiss,	To enrich you
And no more;	I'll restore
If so be, this	For that one, two
Makes you poor,	Thousand score.

On the other hand, the following line from Noyes's *The Highwayman* is an extended metaphor by the second of these criteria but not by the first;

The moon was a ghostly galleon tossed upon cloudy seas.

Herrick's poem extends for eight lines a simple Form 2 metaphor in which a kiss is likened to money. The single line from Noyes involves two related metaphors, one in which the moon is compared to a galleon, and a second in which the clouds are compared to seas. In the rest of this discussion I shall use the term *extended metaphor* to refer to this latter type.

A *complex metaphor* is one in which the literal meaning is expressed through more than one figurative term and the figurative terms belong to different figurative contexts. The line just quoted from Noyes is a complex metaphor as well as an extended metaphor, because, in addition to the two metaphors cited, it contains a third metaphor in which the moon, already compared to a galleon, is simultaneously compared to a ghost, and the ghost image belongs to a different figurative context than the galleon-seas image.

A complex metaphor is not to be confused with a series of simple metaphors in which the literal term is named only once. In the familiar "sleep" passage in *Macbeth* (act II, scene II), for instance, or in the following lines from George Walter Thornbury's *The Jester's Sermon*, each metaphorical comparison is completed before the next one is begun:

> Man's life is but a jest,
> A dream, a shadow, bubble, air, a vapor at the best.

In this example the phrase "man's life is but" may be understood as preceding each noun in the list. In a complex metaphor the disparate figurative terms are all part of one image, not of a series of images. For instance, in Browning's *Meeting at Night* the speaker, as he rows to shore, sees

> the startled little waves that leap
> In fiery ringlets from their sleep.

Here the literal term—"waves"—is expressed through three figurative terms. The words "startled," "leap," and "sleep" compare the waves, unobtrusively, to a person. The word "ringlets" compares them to hair. The adjective "fiery" compares them (as they catch the light of the moon) to flames. The three figurative terms are all part of one metaphor, and they work together to make one image.

A complex metaphor might be called a mixed metaphor except that the term "mixed metaphor" suggests something bad. The truth is that a poet may mix his metaphors as much as he pleases so long as he can get away with it. A "mixed metaphor" is simply an unsuccessful complex metaphor, one in which the figurative terms clash rather than harmonize. I do not know of a logical test by which successful and unsuccessful complex metaphors may be separated. The only test is the imagination of a sensitive reader. I do know that a complex metaphor may be one of the most meaningful devices of poetry. For example, in Robert Frost's *The Tuft of Flowers* the speaker is turning over the grass in a field which has been mowed by a different worker earlier in the morning. The speaker is *alone*—"as all must be," he tells himself, "whether they work together or apart." He then discovers a tuft of flowers which the earlier worker had spared while mowing everything around it:

> A leaping tongue of bloom the scythe had spared
> Beside a reedy brook the scythe had bared.

The literal term is "tuft of flowers" or "bloom," and the figurative term—suggested by the noun "tongue," the participle "leaping," and the sound structure of "bloom"—is a flame. At this point the metaphor is perceived as a simple one, for the figurative implications of "tongue" remain dormant: a "tongue of flame" is a dead metaphor, like the "leg of a table" or the "arm of a chair." Six lines further on, however, when the speaker says that in the tuft of flowers he has lit upon a "message from the dawn," the dead metaphor leaps to life: the "tongue of bloom" has spoken, and it enables the speaker, in fancy, to hold "brotherly speech" with the earlier worker. The tongue and the flame are now seen to be separately figurative, and the metaphor to be a complex one. Structurally, this complex metaphor provides the turning point of the poem, for the "message" of the tuft of flowers changes the attitude of the speaker, who concludes that men work *together*, "whether they work together or apart."

It should by now be apparent that figurative language has a protean quality: it shifts shapes with lightning-like rapidity. In the rest of this section I wish to discuss some of these shape-shiftings.

First, in metaphors that are even slightly extended, there may be among the subsidiary metaphors more than one of the four forms:

The welkin had full niggardly inclosed
In coffer of dim clouds his silver groats.

Sidney: Arcadia

The controlling image in these two lines is a Form 2 metaphor in which the sky is compared to a miser. It is supported, however, by a Form 1 metaphor in which the clouds are represented as a coffer, and by a Form 3 metaphor in which the stars become silver coins. Even a simple, non-extended, metaphor may involve more than one of the four forms.

Ye quenchless stars! so eloquently bright.

Earlier in the essay I over-simply presented this line as a Form 2 metaphor in which the adverb "eloquently" personifies the stars. Upon reflection, however, it becomes apparent that even more important here is a Form 4 metaphor in which shining is compared to speech. The literal term is presented in the adjective "bright," the figurative term in the adverb "eloquently." Neither the literal nor the figurative term in this comparison is named.

Just as a single image may combine more than one form of metaphor, so it may combine more than one figure of speech:

I am soft sift
In an hour glass.

Hopkins: The Wreck of the Deutschland

In Hopkins' lines "sift" is a metonymy for sand, which in turn is the figurative term of a metaphor of which the literal term is "I."

The tower said, "One!"
And then a steeple.
They spoke to themselves . . .
                                    Frost: *I Will Sing You One-O*

In this example "tower" and "steeple" are both personified; at the same time both are metonymies for a clock.

No, it took all the snows that clung
To the low roof over his bed,
Beginning when he was young,
To induce the one snow on his head.
                        Frost: *They Were Welcome to Their Belief*

In this passage "snows" and "snow" are both figurative terms, but they have different referents, and are different figures. "Snows" is a metonymy for winters, which in turn is a metonymy for years, or time; "snow" is the figurative term of a Form 3 metaphor whose literal term is white hair. And so it goes. A passage may be at once ironical and metaphorical. The resolution of a paradox may depend on seeing that one of its contradictory terms is a metaphor. Metaphor and simile are constantly sliding into each other:

O thou are fairer than the evening air
Clad in the beauty of a thousand stars!
                                    Marlowe: *Dr. Faustus*

The comparison of a woman to the evening air is simile, but the evening air is immediately personified because it is "clad," and the stars are the literal term of a Form 2 metaphor in which the figurative term is a garment.

Even figurative and literal language may exist side by side in strange ways:

The hand that signed the paper felled a city;
Five sovereign fingers taxed the breath,
Doubled the globe of dead and halved a country;
These five kings did a king to death.
                        Dylan Thomas: *The Hand That Signed the Paper*

In this passage the "five kings" are metaphorical, whereas "king" three words later is literal. The sudden shift from figurative to literal is what gives the line its "play," its vitality.

Let me conclude this section by examining a whole poem:

There is a garden in her face,
Where roses and white lilies grow;
A heavenly paradise is that place,
Wherein all pleasant fruits do flow.
There cherries grow which none may buy
Till cherry-ripe themselves do cry.

Those cherries fairly do enclose
Of orient pearl a double row,
Which when her lovely laughter shows,
They look like rosebuds filled with snow.
Yet them nor peer nor prince can buy,
Till cherry-ripe themselves do cry.

Her eyes like angels watch them still;
Her brows like bended bows do stand,
Threat'ning with piercing frowns to kill
All that attempt with eye or hand
Those sacred cherries to come nigh,
Till cherry-ripe themselves do cry.

Thomas Campion

The controlling image in the poem is a Form 1 metaphor in which the lady's face is compared to a garden. This is developed in the first stanza through a series of subsidiary Form 3 metaphors. Within the garden are roses and white lilies (the colors of her complexion), pleasant fruits (matured and appealing features), and cherries (her lips).

In the second stanza the garden metaphor is made complex by the introduction of another Form 3 metaphor, in which the lady's teeth are compared to pearls. Through similes the lady's teeth are also compared to snow and her lips to rosebuds, images which return the poem to the garden metaphor. (It should be noticed, however, that neither lips nor teeth are mentioned in the poem: the literal terms of the simile are represented by the figurative terms of the metaphor; so we have here what might be called a Form 3 simile, if that is possible.)

In the third stanza we find that the garden is inhabited. The lady's eyes are compared to angels through simile, and her brows to bended bows. At the same time that the brows are compared to bows, however, they are also personified (since they "threaten") through a Form 2 metaphor. In the development of this simile, another Form 2 metaphor is evolved, in which "piercing frowns" are compared to arrows.

The most remarkable metaphorical development of this poem, however, is in its refrain. The plain sense of these lines, as I read them, is that no one may kiss the lady's lips until she herself issues the invitation or at least gives her consent. This plain sense is rendered through three Form 4 metaphors. Kisses are compared to the purchase of cherries. An invitation or consent to a kiss is compared to calling out "Cherry-ripe." And the lips that call out "Cherry-ripe" are not only cherries to be sold but the cherry-vendor who sells them. Campion's poem thus involves all four forms of metaphor as well as simile. Its basic metaphor is both extended and complex. The poem as a whole is a combination of logically inconsistent but poetically consistent ideas which results in something altogether charming.

7

It might be supposed that the series of figures beginning with simile and ascending through metaphors of Forms 1, 2, 3, and 4 offer a progressively greater difficulty for the reader, but this is only partially true. Actually, there is a much greater variance among examples in a single class than there is among representative examples of the different classes. It is probable, for instance, that the simile which opens Eliot's *Love Song of J. Alfred Prufrock*—

> Let us go then, you and I,
> When the evening is spread out against the sky
> Like a patient etherized upon a table—

has troubled many readers who have not had a moment's difficulty with Emily Dickinson's extended Form 4 metaphor "I like to see it lap the miles." The reason is that the difficulty of a figure of speech depends upon a number of considerations.

Considering problems of interpretation from the viewpoint of metaphorical analysis only, there are four basic questions that must be answered: 1) Is the passage metaphorical or literal? 2) What two things are being compared? 3) Which is the literal and which the figurative term? 4) What are the grounds of the comparison?

The first of these questions is the most hazardous, for the danger is that it may not get asked. Unless a reader recognizes a passage as metaphorical, he will have no reason to ask the other questions in this list. The difficulty arises with Form 3 and Form 4 metaphors, which may often be mistaken for literal statements. Many students, confronted with Emily Dickinson's poem for the first time, read it simply as being about a horse. Form 3 and Form 4 metaphors vary considerably in the number and subtlety of clues presented that they are non-literal.

The second and third of these questions arise with metaphors of Forms 2, 3, and 4. Obviously, if only the literal term is stated, the figurative term must be inferred; if only the figurative term is stated, the literal term must be inferred; if neither is stated, both must be inferred. And, again, there is much variation in the identity of the suppressed terms. Metaphors in which the literal term is suppressed will be more hazardous than those in which the figurative term is suppressed, for the literal term is more important to a passage's plain sense. Occasionally, even when he has identified the two things being compared, a reader will fail to recognize which is the literal term and which the figurative. The fourth of these questions arises with all similes and metaphors. The two things being compared may be obviously alike or obscurely alike. This is why Eliot's simile in *Prufrock* may be more difficult than Dickinson's Form 4 metaphor. Once the literal and figurative terms have been identified, Emily Dickinson's poem offers little difficulty. The literal and figurative terms of Eliot's simile are obvious, but the likenesses between them may baffle a reader coming to Eliot's poetry for the first time.

In the rest of this section I should like to illustrate the problems raised by the first three questions. Since problems raised by the fourth question are unrelated to the form of metaphor used, I shall not address myself to them specifically.

The problem of recognizing a passage as metaphorical has already been discussed in connection with a line from *Romeo and Juliet*. There the issue was resolved by reference to the context. The problem becomes more acute when metaphors of this type are extended throughout a poem, for then there is no surrounding context to refer to, and understanding of the whole poem depends upon recognition of the metaphor. A reader who missed the metaphor in "Night's candles are burnt out" would suffer very little in his understanding of *Romeo and Juliet*. Quite otherwise would be the case of a reader who missed the metaphor in Melville's *The Night-March* (see discussion on pages 12-15) or in the following poem by Emily Dickinson

> The snow that never drifts—
> The transient, fragrant snow
> That comes a single time a year—
> Is softly driving now;
>
> So thorough in the tree
> At night beneath the star
> That it was February's self
> Experience would swear;
>
> Like winter as a face
> We stern and former knew
> Repaired of all but loneliness
> By nature's alibi.
>
> Were every storm so spice
> The value could not be;
> We buy with contrast—pang is good
> As near as memory.

The poet's editors, when they included this poem in *Bolts of Melody*, interpreted the snow as literal and classified the poem as a late winter poem. Actually it is not about snow at all, but about a fall of white blossoms in late spring.* The poem is an extended Form 3 metaphor.

Even when it is suspected that a passage may be metaphorical, it can be difficult, with a Form 3 metaphor, to determine whether or not it is actually so. The problem is illustrated vividly by a controversy waged in the pages of *The Explicator* a number of years ago over the proper reading of Housman's *Loveliest of Trees*. The poem begins:

> Loveliest of trees, the cherry now
> Is hung with bloom along the bough
> And stands about the woodland ride,
> Wearing white for Eastertide.

It ends:

> And since to look at things in bloom
> Fifty springs are little room,
> About the woodlands I will go
> To see the cherry hung with snow.

The snow in this poem is a Form 3 metaphor like that in Emily Dickinson's poem: its literal meaning is white blossoms. But some five scholars and critics in *The Explicator*, recognizing the possibility of this interpretation, argued seriously that this snow is literal.†

Once a passage has been diagnosed as metaphorical, there still remains the problem of determining what two things are being compared. A Form 4 metaphor offers two opportunities for going wrong. Emily Dickinson's poem about the train has caused disagreement as to both its literal and figurative terms. Any teacher who presents this poem for analysis to a class will find, among students who have not encountered it before, considerable bafflement as to what the poem is about. In addition to those who read the poem literally as about a horse, I have had students tell me that it is about a river, a road, poetry and death. Scholars, on the other hand, have had little difficulty with what the poem is about, but have differed about the figurative element. The usual interpretation is that the image throughout is, as Charles R. Anderson puts it, of "a fabulous horse." Some critics, however, have suggested that the figurative term is a monstrous dragon; that it is a mythological beast at first catlike and later horselike; that it is a "zoological exhibit of cat, dragon, *and* horse"; or that it changes progressively from cat to hunting dog to colt to horse as the train approaches the viewer. Although I agree with the first of these interpretations, my purpose here is not to argue a case but simply to illustrate the difficulties.

*Ralph Marcellino corrects this misreading in *The Explicator*, vol 13 (April 1955), item 36.
†For a summary see my discussion in *The CEA Critic*, vol 35 (November 1972), pp. 26-27.

When literal and figurative terms have been correctly identified, there still remains the problem of determining which is which. This problem rarely causes difficulty, but occasionally it does. The point was forcefully brought to my attention recently in a graduate seminar discussion of A. D. Hope's poem *The Brides*. The poem begins as follows:

Down the assembly line they roll and pass
Complete at last, a miracle of design;
Their chromium fenders, the unbreakable glass,
The fashionable curve, the air-flow line.

The whole poem, which continues for five more stanzas, is in fact an extended Form 2 metaphor in which brides are compared to new automobiles. At the end of the poem one of them is driven off by her purchaser. My students had no difficulty at all in identifying the two things being compared, and in seeing that the poem is satirical; but they divided as to whether the poem is a satire against society's preparing girls for marriage as if they were automobiles for purchase, or against men's falling in love with automobiles and treating them as if they were brides.

8

What advantages has my system of classifying metaphors?

First, I think, it has advantages of simplicity and naturalness. I have discussed these points briefly in my remarks on a metaphor from Boswell. They are illustrated even better by the example from Francis Thompson:

The tawny-hided desert crouches watching her.

This line contains three figurative expressions—"tawny-hided," "crouches," and "watching." By a grammatical analysis we should have to consider them as three separate metaphors. The adjective is the easiest. "Tawny-hided" means "having a dull yellowish surface" or "sandy." The verb is somewhat more difficult. "Crouches," implying a readiness to spring, means here "extends around her full of menace." For the participle—"watching"—it is almost impossible to find a literal equivalent. We can say easily enough what is meant: that the girl is in danger, that if she makes the slightest slip she will be overcome by heat prostration, thirst, or savage attack. But it seems impossible to translate "watching" satisfactorily into a literal equivalent. And surely this analysis avoids the key image. Is it not simpler and more natural to see this image in terms of one metaphor rather than three? What two things are being compared? we ask. Answer: the desert and a lion. Then we ask, in what ways is the desert like a lion? Answer: Both are dullish yellow in color; both are treacherous; both may cause terrible death. In answering this second question we have brought out, but more naturally and easily, all the equivalences we struggled for so laboriously through a grammatical analysis.

The example cited from *All's Well That Ends Well* further shows the difficulties of grammatical analysis:

> For we are old, and in our quick'st degrees
> The inaudible and noiseless foot of Time
> Steals ere we can effect them.

In this passage there are two figurative expressions: "foot" and "steals." "Steals" may be translated as "passes unobtrusively or unnoticed." But what do we do with "foot"? As remarked earlier, it is figurative, yet it has no literal equivalent. The metaphor in this passage likens Time to a person, and "foot" is an elaboration of its figurative term, not a figurative term in itself. It *belongs* to a metaphor without *being* a metaphor. Elaboration of the figurative term is seen most markedly in Homeric simile, but it is a phenomenon of metaphor in all ages.

A second advantage of the proposed scheme is that it gives us a much clearer conceptual framework for comparing simile and metaphor. Critics have long been given to making sweeping generalizations about the differences between simile and metaphor, as to both their effects and their effectiveness. But they have not always been clear about what they were comparing. Simile is in fact closely comparable only to Form 1 metaphor. In each of them both literal and figurative terms are named, and the only significant difference is the use in simile of some word such as "like" or "as" which makes the comparison overt. Simile indeed might be logically classed as a subspecies of Form 1 metaphor, for the likenesses are more important than the difference. Certainly, however, in comparisons between simile and other forms of metaphor, the use of "like" or "as" in simile is the least important difference. It is not true, as textbooks may sometimes lead one to believe, that any metaphor can be converted to a simile simply by the introduction of "like" or "as."

Third, the scheme presents a simple conceptual framework for teaching metaphor and for clarifying the ways in which metaphor works. Though no conceivable method of teaching metaphor will prevent the kinds of misinterpretation illustrated in the previous section of this essay, yet possession of this conceptual scheme may cut down on a few misreadings. Its advantage is that it gives the student a notion of what to expect. If he knows what he may expect, he is better prepared to deal with what he finds. The explorer of the realms of gold, like any other explorer, is less likely to suffer shipwreck if he sails forth provided with compass and sextant.

A Look at Rhythm and Meter

Rhythm is a quality of all high art. There is rhythm in painting and sculpture in that certain curves and dips recur and repeat each other. There is rhythm in the dance in the graceful flow of motion from finger to toe, involving every part of the body in patterned movement. There is rhythm, obviously, in music, beaten out perhaps by the drum and inviting us to tap our feet in time to it. There is rhythm in well-written prose, where the lines flow gracefully and in cadenced movement rather than proceeding jerkily or spasmodically. In fact, there is rhythm in almost all human activity when it is done well, whether it be rowing a boat, skipping rope, swinging an ax, raking a yard, or doing some repetitive action on an assembly line. The poor performer operates jerkily and clumsily, tripping over the rope or "catching crabs" with the oar, while the good performer operates smoothly, with a certain recurrent and measured motion in space and time. There is rhythm even in breathing—the act of life itself. When death is near, the breath becomes jerky and spasmodic.

All good poetry is rhythmical. A major part of the best poetry has also been metrical: composed in meter. Meter is ordered rhythm. In all words or phrases of more than one syllable, certain syllables are given heavier stress in pronunciation than others. Meter arranges these stresses so that they recur with a certain regularity. It separates the stresses with a more or less fixed number of unstressed syllables, and it may also allot a fixed number of stresses to each line. Meter thus imposes order on language that is spoken or read aloud. It gives language an oral and aural pattern. *Meter* means *measure*, and metrical language can be measured —by the number of syllables in the foot (the basic unit, containing one beat) and the number of feet in the line.

Perfect regularity in meter is not ordinarily to be desired. The uniformity of "tick-tock, tick-tock" or "pocketa-pocketa-pocketa" suggests machinery rather than the organic rhythms of life. A poem which continued long with such mechanical regularity would soon become monotonous. The good poet seeks repetition with variety. He avoids the perfect regularity of machinery, on the one hand, and the complete variety of chaos, on the other. The basic meter which the poet chooses is therefore something like the drumbeat in music around which the instruments weave their various melodies. The reader is always aware of this basic pattern (the *expected* rhythm), though what he actually hears (the *heard* rhythm) sometimes confirms and sometimes departs from it. If the heard rhythm departs too far or too long from the expected rhythm, the expected rhythm vanishes and the verse turns into prose. If the heard rhythm confirms the expected rhythm too rigidly, the verse becomes tedious and mechanical. But there is another reason for desiring variety within a pattern. Meter acquires its expressive power largely by its departures from perfect regularity.

Meter has at least three uses for the poet: First, it is pleasurable for its own sake, as evidenced by the universal pleasure that children take in purely nonsense verses. Second, if skillfully used, it serves as an emotional stimulus and may heighten the reader's attention to what the poem is saying. Third, again if skillfully used, meter can increase the expressive power of language by adapting the sound and movement of the language to its content. In other words, the poet, by his choice of basic meter and by his departures from perfect regularity within that meter, can reinforce the *meanings* of the words he is using. He can do this in two ways: by making the meter emphasize words that are important to the poem's meaning, and by making the movement of the lines correspond to the mood or movement of their content.

In our first reading of the following poem, we should become aware of a basic metrical pattern. But we also note that the author sometimes departs from that pattern.

SAY NOT THE STRUGGLE NOUGHT AVAILETH

Say not the struggle nought availeth,
   The labor and the wounds are vain,
The enemy faints not, nor faileth,
   And as things have been they remain.

If hopes were dupes, fears may be liars;   5
   It may be, in yon smoke concealed,
Your comrades chase e'en now the fliers,
   And, but for you, possess the field.

For while the tired waves, vainly breaking
   Seem here no painful inch to gain,   10
Far back, through creeks and inlets making,
   Comes silent, flooding in, the main.

And not by eastern windows only,
   When daylight comes, comes in the light,
In front, the sun climbs slow, how slowly,   15
   But westward, look, the land is bright.

       Arthur Hugh Clough

Now we are ready for a closer look at the metrical pattern. *Say Not the Strug-*

gle Nought Availeth might be printed like this for the sake of metrical analysis:*

say NOT / the STRUG- / gle NOUGHT / a-VAIL- / eth,
The LA- / bor AND/ the WOUNDS / are VAIN, /
the EN- / e-MY / FAINTS NOT, / nor FAIL- / eth,
and AS / things HAVE / been THEY / re-MAIN. /

if HOPES / were DUPES, / FEARS may / be LI- / ars;   5
it MAY / be, IN / YON SMOKE / con-CEALED, /
your COM- / rades CHASE / e'en NOW / the FLI- / ers,
and, BUT / for YOU, / pos-SESS / the FIELD. /

for WHILE / the TIRED / WAVES, VAIN- / ly BREAK- / ing,
seem HERE / no PAIN- / ful INCH / to GAIN, /   10
FAR BACK, / through CREEKS / and IN- / lets MAK- / ing,
comes SI- / lent, FLOOD- / ing IN, / the MAIN. /

and NOT / by EAST- / ern WIN- / dows ON- / ly,
when DAY- / light COMES, / comes IN / the LIGHT, /
in FRONT, / the SUN / CLIMBS SLOW, / HOW SLOW- / ly,   15
but WEST- / ward, LOOK, / the LAND / is BRIGHT. /

The basic meter used by Clough is one in which every other syllable in a line is stressed. The foot therefore may be said to contain two syllables, with the stress on the second. In addition, Clough has written his poem in four-line stanzas, in which each line contains four feet, with an extra unstressed syllable left over at the end of the first and third lines of each stanza. We may indicate the basic pattern (the *expected* rhythm) thus:

xX / xX / xX / xX / x
xX / xX / xX / xX /
xX / xX / xX / xX / x
xX / xX / xX / xX /

But Clough has skillfully varied this basic pattern.

The poet can vary his meter in several ways. He can introduce grammatical or rhetorical pauses into his lines. More than half of Clough's lines contain internal commas, demanding minute pauses which prevent the *heard* rhythm from going "click-clack, click-clack." Next, the poet can introduce variety of phrasing so that the phrasal pattern is at variance with the metrical pattern. In Clough's

---

*Metrical analysis (or *scansion*) is not an exact science, and different readers may legitimately disagree about details. Another reader might not scan the third and sixth lines as I have done, or the first foot in line 11. There might be other disagreements, also, but about the major features there should be agreement.

There are different devices for indicating scansion. The device used here, of capitalizing the stressed syllables and of separating the feet with a slash, is only one.

poem no single line shows perfect correspondence of phrasal and metrical pat-tern.In line 7, for instance, the metrical division of the line is:

your com- / rades chase / e'en now / the fli / ers,

but the phrasal division is more like this:

your comrades / chase / e'en now / the fliers.

If Clough had written:

your friends / pursue / e'en now / the fliers,

he would have had a closer correspondence; but he rightly preferred greater variety, with the phrasal pattern playing across the metrical pattern. A further way in which the poet can introduce variety is by varying the degree of stress in his stressed and unstressed syllables. Actually there is seldom *exactly* the same degree of stress on any two syllables, but sometimes the differences are marked. In lines 2 and 3, we have indicated that the stress on "and" and on the third syl-lable of "enemy" is very light by printing these syllables in small capitals rather than large. Finally, the poet may vary his meter by occasionally substituting a different kind of foot from that called for by the pattern. In line 5 of Clough's poem the third foot is inverted, with its stress on the first rather than on the second syllable. In lines 3, 6, 9, 11, and 15 Clough has introduced feet in which the stress is equally distributed over *both* syllables. If we tap out the meter of the poem, we see that these lines have four feet like the others; but each has one foot in which one syllable is stressed almost equally with the other. The effect of

for WHILE / the TIRED / WAVES, VAIN- / ly BREAK- / ing

is quite different from

for WHILE/ the WAVES / so VAIN- / ly BREAK- / ing,

which Clough could have written.

Our poet has thus skillfully varied his basic meter, avoiding monotony. But, even more important, by his departures from perfect regularity he has reinforced his meaning. In line 16, for example, the grammatical pauses on either side of "look" have the effect of isolating that word and giving it an increased emphasis appropriate to its function in the dramatic context of the poem. In line 5 the inversion of stress in the third foot, following a grammatical pause, puts a very heavy emphasis on "fears" which again is appropriate to the meaning. The line is much more forceful than if Clough had written

if HOPES / were DUPES, / so FEARS / may CO- / zen.

In line 3 the phrase "faints not," distributing its stress over both syllables and following the very light stress on the final syllable of "enemy," receives a very much heavier emphasis than the idea it expresses would have received if Clough had written

the FOE- / man FAINT- / eth NOT, / nor FAIL- / eth.

In these examples the meaning has been reinforced by the emphasis which meter has placed on words or phrases important to the meaning. An even more dramatic reinforcement of meaning occurs when the metrical *movement* of the line is made to correspond to the mood or movement indicated by the content. In line 15 Clough could have written a metrically regular line:

in FRONT / the SUN / a-RIS- / es SLOW- / ly.

But this line, so written, *moves* rather fast. Accordingly, Clough has slowed the line down in several ways. First, he has introduced two feet in which the stress is divided between the two syllables. (Whenever unstressed syllables occur together, the effect is to speed the line up; whenever stressed syllables occur together, the effect is to slow it down. Clough here forces five stressed syllables together.) Second, he has introduced two grammatical pauses, indicated by the commas. Third, he has thrust sounds together which are difficult to pronounce quickly. (The three syllables of "arises" glide easily off the tongue, but the sounds of "climbs slow how" cannot be uttered swiftly.) In making these changes in movement, Clough has repeated the key word "slow." The result is a line in which sound and movement correspond beautifully to meaning:

in FRONT, / the SUN / CLIMBS SLOW, / HOW SLOW- / ly.

A similar effect is achieved in line 9.

There are three basic meters in English verse. In the first (illustrated by *Say Not the Struggle Nought Availeth*), the stresses fall on every other syllable. This may be called *duple* meter, for there are two syllables in the foot.* In the second, the stresses fall on every third syllable. This meter (illustrated by *if everything happens that can't be done*, page 70) may be called *triple* meter, for it has three syllables in each foot.† In the third kind of meter, the stresses again fall on every other syllable, but the stresses themselves are alternated between light and heavy. This meter, called *dipodic* ("two-footed"), may be considered to have a four-

---

*If the stress falls on the second syllable, the meter is called *iambic*; if on the first, *trochaic*. Actually the distinction between iambic and trochaic is arbitrary, depending on whether the lines begin and end on stressed or unstressed syllables. *Say Not the Struggle Nought Availeth* is iambic because the even-numbered lines begin on unstressed and end on stressed syllables; but if it had consisted of the odd-numbered lines only, it could be construed as either iambic or trochaic. Either way, there would be one unaccented syllable left over, either at the end or at the beginning of the line.

†The meter is called *dactylic* if the stress falls on the first syllable of the three; *anapestic*, if on the last syllable. But again, the distinction is arbitrary.

syllable foot. The following poem is an example:

TOMORROW

Oh yesterday the cutting edge drank thirstily and deep,
The upland outlaws ringed us in and herded us as sheep,
They drove us from the stricken field and bayed us into keep;
    But tomorrow,
    By the living God, we'll try the game again!

Oh yesterday our little troop was ridden through and through,
Our swaying, tattered pennons fled, a broken, beaten few,
And all a summer afternoon they hunted us and slew;
    But tomorrow,
    By the living God, we'll try the game again!

And here upon the turret-top the bale-fire glowers red,
The wake-lights burn and drip about our hacked, disfigured dead,
And many a broken heart is here and many a broken head;
    But tomorrow,
    By the living God, we'll try the game again!

                John Masefield

A metrical analysis of the first stanza reveals the alternating pattern:

oh YES-/ ter-DAY the CUT-/ ting EDGE drank THIRST- / i-LY and DEEP, /
the UP- / land OUT- laws RINGED / us IN and HERD- / ed US as SHEEP, /
they DROVE / us FROM the STRICK- / en FIELD and BAYED / us IN-to
KEEP; /
    but to-MOR- / row,
    BY the LIV- / ing GOD, we'll TRY / the GAME a-GAIN!*

Of the three meters mentioned, the first is by far the most common, the second
is used occasionally, and the third appears infrequently.

Each of these meters, abstractly considered, has its own effect. Triple meter,
other things being equal, is swifter than duple meter (since it has more un-
stressed syllables). Dipodic meter is ordinarily swifter yet (because of the lightness
of the lightly stressed syllable) and, in addition, has a pronounced lilt (because
of the alternation of light and heavy stresses). But a skillful poet can alter the
effect of any meter by the way he uses it. He can slow down a swift meter or

*Of the three basic meters, dipodic allows the most variation and is the most difficult to
analyze. Considerable subjectivity enters into determining whether a stress should be indica-
ted as light or heavy, and the reader is at liberty to quarrel with the scansion given here. An
absolute alternation of light and heavy stresses throughout the poem is not essential so long
as it is frequent enough to establish a sense of the pattern in the reader's mind.

speed up a slow one. He can introduce lilt into a steady meter, or he can steady up a lilting one. He thus has enormous resources at his disposal, much greater than does the writer of prose or of unmetrical verse. He can reinforce his mood and meaning both by his choice of meter and by his local handling of it.*

Arthur Hugh Clough, for a relatively solemn subject, chose the slowest of the three basic meters and slowed it down even further by his handling of it. E. E. Cummings, in *if everything happens that can't be done*, has a different problem. His subject is reciprocated love, and his mood is ecstatic joy. For this content he appropriately chooses a swift triple meter and uses it in such a way as to make it dance.

IF EVERYTHING HAPPENS THAT CAN'T BE DONE

if everything happens that can't be done
(and anything's righter
than books
could plan)
the stupidest teacher will almost guess
(with a run
skip
around we go yes)
there's nothing as something as one

one hasn't a why or because or although
(and buds know better
than books
don't grow)
one's anything old being everything new
(with a what
which
around we come who)
one's everyanything so

so world is a leaf so tree is a bough
(and birds sing sweeter
than books
tell how)

---

*The number of feet in a line also influences the effect of a meter. Other things being equal, trimeter (three feet to the line) and tetrameter (four feet to the line) are likely to be more lyrical or song-like in effect than pentameter (five feet to the line), which, however, has more natural dignity. But increasing line-length does not inevitably mean increasing dignity, for the hexameter (six-foot) line tends, in the reading, to divide in the middle and become in effect two trimeter lines. Again, however, these general tendencies may be greatly modified or even reversed in specific poems. The possibilities for different metrical effects are numberless.

so here is away and so your is a my
(with a down
up
around again fly)
forever was never till now

now i love you and you love me
(and books are shuter
than books
can be)
and deep in the high that does nothing but fall
(with a shout
each
around we go all)
there's somebody calling who's we

we're anything brighter than even the sun
(we're everything greater
than books
might mean)
we're everyanything more than believe
(with a spin
leap
alive we're alive)
we're wonderful one times one

     E. E. Cummings

Before scanning Cummings' poem, we should perhaps say a word about its content. E. E. Cummings is a romantic poet for whom, if there is anything more wonderful than being a live individual with a heart and feelings of one's own (a "one"; not a cipher, a nonentity, a conformist, an emotionally dead person), it is being one of *two* individuals (two "ones") who achieve identity through love. For Cummings, being alive, or being an individual (and therefore capable of love), is a function of feeling, not of intellect. The analytic reason (symbolized throughout the poem by "books" and in stanza two by analytic terms such as "why," "because," and "although") for Cummings deadens and kills, whereas feeling (symbolized by "buds" and "birds" and "trees") enlivens and vitalizes ("buds know better than books" and "books don't grow," to expand Cummings' telescoped phrase). The consummation of natural feeling comes with the mutually realized love of two individuals ("one times one"). When such miracles happen (when "everything happens that can't be done"), as they regularly do in the spring, then even "the stupidest teacher" (representing the intellect again) will dimly guess the miraculousness of individuality, feeling, spring, life, and love.

Cummings has constructed his poem on an intricate pattern. Each stanza is linked to the one that follows by the fact that the last word in one is the first word in the next. They thus hold on to each other like persons holding hands. Lines 2-4 of each stanza contain a parenthesis in which life and feeling are contrasted with intellect ("books"). Lines 6-8 of each stanza contain a second parenthesis which indicates that the participants in the poem are engaged in a joyous dance. Each stanza is additionally organized by a pattern of approximate rhyme in which the first line rhymes with the fourth and the ninth, and the fifth with the eighth. The basic meter is triple, with four feet in the first line, two in the second, one in the third, one in the fourth, four in the fifth, one in the sixth, one in the seventh, two in the eighth, and three in the ninth.

It may be noticed that if the lines within parentheses had been printed as single lines, then every line would be a rhyming one, and the stanzaic structure would be simplified. In this case the first stanza would scan thus:

if EV- / ery-thing HAP- / pens that CAN'T / be DONE /
(and AN- / y-thing's RIGHT- / er than BOOKS / could PLAN) /
the STU- / pid-est TEACH- / er will AL- / most GUESS /
(with a RUN / SKIP / a-ROUND / we go YES) /
there's NOTH- / ing as SOME- / thing as ONE / *

Printed this way, the rhyme scheme emerges as *a-a-b-b-a*, and the basic metrical pattern is seen to have four feet in the first four lines and three feet in the fifth, thus:

xxX / xxX / xxX / xxX /
xxX / xxX / xxX / xxX /
xxX / xxX / xxX / xxX /
xxX / xxX / xxX / xxX /
xxX / xxX / xxX /

Cummings varies this basic meter by the use of numerous substitute feet. One or more duple feet replace the basic triple foot in every line of the poem (as printed above). Without appreciably slowing the meter down, these substitutes introduce a slight irregularity, a note of spontaneity, a bit of a lilt, a variety of movement which reinforces the sense of vitality, the feeling of joyousness expressed by the content. If Cummings had written

if a LOT / of things HAP- / pen than CAN- / not be DONE /
and ex-IS- / tence is RIGHT- / er than BOOKS / can de-VISE /,

---

*Some words (e. g., "fire") may be pronounced as either one syllable or two and will be pronounced one way or the other depending on the metrical context. "Everything" in the first line of this poem is pronounced in three syllables, as if it were "ev'rything." On the other hand, in the last line of the second stanza (and in the middle line of the last stanza), it is pronounced as four syllables:

one's EV- / er-y-AN- / y-thing SO.

the effect would have been more that of a mechanical race. The most interesting substitution, however, is in the fourth line (as printed above). Here, between two triple feet are substituted a monosyllabic and a duple foot. These lines, in their content, describe a joyous spontaneous dance. The variety of movement produced by these substitutions puts the very swirl and movement of the dance into the meter of the poem. The line, in fact, *skips* in its movement exactly where the content calls for a skip. We can almost hear the participants' feet touching the ground rapidly on "with a run," leaping into the air on "skip," touching ground and resuming their run on "around we go yes." And now also we see why Cummings has broken down line 4 into three smaller units. The additional pauses thus introduced into the line, by increasing its variety, increase its dance-like movement. This dance motion is seen also in the way line 2 is actually divided. The effect of

and AN- / y-thing's RIGHT- / er
than BOOKS /
could PLAN /

is different and much more dance-like than

and AN- / y-thing's RIGHT- / er than BOOKS / could PLAN /.

Thus the feeling of ecstatic joy produced by Cummings's poem is almost as much a result of the meter and the poet's handling of it as it is of the words themselves. But one line of the poem demands further examination. The first line of the fourth stanza is the key line for understanding what the poem is about. Here the poem states its subject: the cause for all this joy and dancing. But this line also is unique in having four duple feet:

now I / love YOU / and YOU / love ME.

This is the *only* line in the entire poem (as printed above) without a single triple foot. The effect is to slow down the line and to give it special emphasis. Again the meter underscores the meaning.

We need not suppose that a poet *consciously* plans all his metrical effects. Poems are written, often at white heat, at both the conscious and unconscious levels of the mind. The poet in the process of composition no more thinks about duple or triple or monosyllabic feet than a star halfback during a broken-field run thinks about where he is going to put his foot down next and when he is going to twist his hip. His skill is, nevertheless, not accidental. It is the product of training and natural ability. The poet thinks with his whole mind, not just the conscious portion of it.

Not all good poetry is metrical, of course. Much good poetry since Whitman has been written in *free verse*. Free verse differs from rhythmical prose in its use of an additional rhythmical unit—the line. Just as Cummings produced a different effect in meter by breaking down one line into three, so free verse has a different effect than it would have if its lines were allowed to run on to the margin of the page as in prose. In writing free verse, the poet sacrifices the advantages that inhere in meter, but gains greater freedom and variety. In addition, the best free verse is likely to have, in T. S. Eliot's phrase, "the ghost of a meter" behind it. The relative merits of free verse and meter have been the subject of spirited controversy, which need not concern us here. The important fact for us is that great poetry has been written in both media.

When Form and Content Kiss / Intention Made the Bliss: An Exercise in the Sonnet Form

Romeo: If I profane with my unworthiest hand
           This holy shrine, the gentle sin is this;
           My lips, two blushing pilgrims, ready stand
           To smooth that rough touch with a tender kiss.
Juliet: Good pilgrim, you do wrong your hand too much,
           Which mannerly devotion shows in this;
           For saints have hands that pilgrim's hands do touch,
           And palm to palm is holy palmers' kiss.
Romeo: Have not saints lips, and holy palmers too?
Juliet: Ay, pilgrim, lips that they must use in prayer.
Romeo: O! then, dear saint, let lips do what hands do;
           They pray, Grant thou, lest faith turn to despair.
Juliet: Saints do not move, though grant for prayers' sake.
Romeo: Then move not, while my prayers' effect I take.

Problem

The foregoing 14 lines are excerpted from act I, scene V of Shakespeare's *Romeo and Juliet*. They are not there set off from the rest of the text in any way, and one might not notice their pattern. They have the metrical form (*iambic pentameter*) and the rhyme pattern (*a-b-a-b-c-d-c-d-e-f-e-f-g-g*) of a traditional English sonnet. Since *Romeo and Juliet*, except for a few brief prose passages, is written throughout in iambic pentameter, and since much of it also rhymes, the lines rhyming sometimes alternately and sometimes in pairs, it is not surprising that 14 lines, from a total of almost 3,000, should fall into this pattern. Does the fact that these lines so fall result from coincidence or design?

Answer

That the sonnet-pattern in the rhyming of these 14 lines was the result of a conscious and deliberate intention on Shakespeare's part can be demonstrated with almost complete finality. The steps of the demonstration are three: first, it can be shown that these 14 lines possess a self-contained unity, that they are not simply a fragment with rough edges ripped forcibly from the fabric of the play; second, it can be shown that these lines exhibit an internal organization corresponding to the characteristic internal organization of the English sonnet; third, the appropriateness of the sonnet form to the subject-matter of these lines can be demonstrated, thus establishing the motive (as the mystery writers put it) for Shakespeare's use of the pattern.

The unity of the passage is of four kinds: grammatical, situational, metaphorical and tonal. Obviously the passage begins at the beginning of a sentence, not in the middle of one, and it ends at the end of a sentence, not in the middle of one. It is thus grammatically self-contained—an elementary consideration, but one that would not be true of most 14-line excerpts taken at random from the play. Second, and much more important, these 14 lines cover a self-contained episode or situation; they begin with the first introduction of Romeo and Juliet and end with their first kiss. They thus have a plot of their own, and constitute, in little, a play-within-a-play. Third, the 14 lines are metaphorically unified by a single extended metaphor, one in which a pilgrim, or palmer, is worshipping at the shrine of a saint. Romeo, by virtue of his masquerade costume, is the pilgrim; Juliet, by virtue of her beauty and gentleness, is the saint. Fourth, the religious nature of this metaphor—employing words like "profane, "holy," "shrine," "sin," "pilgrims," "devotion," "saints," "palmers," "prayer," and "faith"—combines with the delicious and graceful wit of the dialogue to give the passage also a unity of tone: a tone of earnest delicacy and delightfully charming gravity which forces us to take seriously an episode we might otherwise take cynically. Romeo, we feel, is not simply a fresh and forward young man and Juliet an easy mark: theirs is genuine love at first sight. "Dear saint, let lips do what hands do" is emotionally a great deal different in meaning from "Gimme a little kiss, honey, won'cha?" In these four ways, then, the passage has a unity which enables it to stand alone—a poem in itself, not a fragment with torn threads.

In addition to forming a self-contained unit, these 14 lines are internally organized like the English sonnet into three groups of four lines each, plus a final couplet. In the first quatrain, Romeo, initiating the basic metaphor, apologizes for taking Juliet's "holy" hand in his unworthy one, but humbly offers to make up for the offence by giving the hand a gentle kiss. In the second quatrain, Juliet reassures Romeo, telling him that he has done no wrong but shows mannerly devotion in taking her hand, for pilgrims quite properly touch saints' hands, and pilgrims "kiss" by clasping hands. She thus at one and the same time encourages Romeo to hold her hand but with maidenly delicacy indicates that there is no need for him to kiss it. In the third quatrain, however, emboldened by this reassurance, Romeo decides to play the long shot and ask for a kiss on the lips. But he puts the request delicately and charmingly. Do not pilgrims and saints have lips as well as hands? he asks. Translated, this means: Since saints and pilgrims (you and I) have lips as well as hands, why should we not kiss with our lips instead of merely with our hands? Juliet, still modest, yet keeping to the metaphor, replies that pilgrims' lips are for praying with. Then Romeo brilliantly seizes his opening: "Let lips do what hands do," he says. The line has two meanings. Hands not only kiss, they also pray. Lips not only pray, they also kiss. So Romeo, shaping his hands into the attitude of prayer, prays also with his lips; but what he prays for is a kiss. In the final couplet, Juliet, not unwillingly defeated in this contest of wit (for what can a saint do when a faithful pilgrim prays to her?) gracefully surrenders; she grants the kiss, thus answering Romeo's prayer. The internal organization of these 14 lines, then, follows the organization of the English sonnet; each quatrain has its proper subject, and the couplet summarizes or climaxes the whole. The first quatrain is Romeo's apology; the second is Juliet's reassurance; the third is the plea; and the couplet is the plea granted—a fitting climax for the sonnet, all lovers will surely agree.

The appropriateness of the sonnet form to the subject of these lines is obvious. In Shakespeare's time especially, the sonnet form was used primarily for the treatment of love. Shakespeare's play is about a pair of "star-crossed lovers." The episode covered in these lines concerns their first introduction to each other and their first kiss. It is a lyrical moment. What more natural than that Shakespeare should turn to the sonnet form, with its associations with love, for treatment of this episode? Shakespeare had already written many poems in the form of the English sonnet and had used it for the treatment of love.

"When form and content kiss, / Intention made the bliss." That Shakespeare deliberately cast these 14 lines into the shape of a sonnet is about as certain as anything of which we can be certain.

How to Read a Poem

In this essay I plan to make a very careful analysis of a poem by A. E. Housman. I have a twofold purpose. First, I want to show something about how to read a poem intelligently—to illustrate procedures one goes through consciously or un-consciously, in reading poetry well. Second, I want to demonstrate that poetry is not language just put down any which way. It is not the random scattering of the poet's impressions, or the spontaneous, disorganized bubbling over of his emotions. Poetry, rather, is the most highly organized kind of language, and it is organized for the single purpose of conveying the greatest amount of meaning. But when I speak of meaning I mean not just intellectual meaning, but also emotional, imaginative, and sensuous meaning. Fullness of meaning is the poet's object, and fullness of meaning requires complexity of organization. In a suc-cessful poem every detail counts: every image, every choice of one word over another, every decision about word order, every nuance of sound, even every accent. Poetry is human speech standing on tiptoe, it is language at its highest stretch. I wish to illustrate how it gets its stretch.

Before I begin my analysis, however, I must warn against two misconceptions that people sometimes get as a result of analysis. In a sense they are opposite misconceptions. One is that poetry ought never to be analyzed. The other is that it must always be analyzed. Let me deal with these misconceptions one at a time.

The first misconception is that to analyze a poem is to kill it. "I hate to have a poem torn to pieces," people say. Such people shrink from examining a poem line by line. They hate to be asked, "What does this line mean? What is the poet doing here?" They prefer to sit back and let the poem wash through their souls.

It is my conviction that such an attitude springs out of intellectual laziness and that it rests on a false analogy. According to this analogy a poem is like a delicate flower. To analyze it is to pull it apart, petal by petal and leaf by leaf. In the process you kill the flower. But poetry is made of hardier stuff. Analyzing a poem is more like taking apart a fine jeweled watch and then putting it to-gether again. The watch runs as well as ever afterward, and the result is that you understand it better and value it more. Or, if a poem must be compared to some-thing natural, like a flower, instead of something made, like a watch, then anal-yzing it is like examining the flower under a magnifying glass. You can examine it leaf, petal, pistil, and stamen, without doing it the slightest damage. You don't have to rip it apart. In fact, you *can't* rip a good poem apart, for the poem is made of elements that always unite again. The hardiest poems in the language are those that have been analyzed oftenest.

But let me drop analogies and testify from experience. My experience is this: analysis may indeed damage or destroy my appreciation of a *bad* poem; it only increases my appreciation of a *good* one. If a poem is empty or phony, analysis exposes its weakness. If a poem is a genuine achievement, analysis reveals the extent of the miracle and can only increase my enjoyment of it.

The second misconception is that a poem is something to be "figured out," a puzzle to be solved, a problem to be approached like a problem in mathematics or a crossword puzzle. This is not true. When we read a poem well, we respond to it instantaneously; its impact is immediate. Reading poetry well is a skill like other skills, like playing the piano well, for instance. The concert pianist, when he sits down to the piano, does not have to think out where he is going to put each finger on the keyboard and in what order or in what combination. He does this as if out of instinct (actually out of long practice), and what he concentrates on is the feeling. Likewise the good reader of poetry, as he reads, does not consciously dissect the meanings of words, or analyze metrical effects. Rather, he *feels* these things, as if instinctively, actually out of long familiarity with language and much practice in reading.

Now let us turn to Housman's poem, first published in 1896 as poem IX in *A Shropshire Lad:*

[1]
On moonlit heath and lonesome bank
    The sheep beside me graze;
And yon the gallows used to clank
    Fast by the four cross ways.

[2]
A careless shepherd once would keep   5
    The flocks by moonlight there,*
And high amongst the glimmering sheep
    The dead man stood on air.

[3]
They hang us now in Shrewsbury jail:
    The whistles blow forlorn,   10
And trains all night groan on the rail
    To men that die at morn.

[4]
There sleeps in Shrewsbury jail to-night,
    Or wakes, as may betide,

*Hanging in chains was called keeping sheep by moonlight. [Housman's note]

A better lad, if things went right,   15
    Than most that sleep outside.

[5]
And naked to the hangman's noose
    The morning clocks will ring
A neck God made for other use
    Than strangling in a string.   20

[6]
And sharp the link of life will snap,
    And dead on air will stand
Heels that held up as straight a chap
    As treads upon the land.

[7]
So here I'll watch the night and wait   25
    To see the morning shine,
When he will hear the stroke of eight
    And not the stroke of nine;

[8]
And wish my friend as sound a sleep
    As lads' I did not know,   30
That shepherded the moonlit sheep
    A hundred years ago.

The first step in understanding a poem is to establish the speaker, the audi-
ence, and the occasion. The speaker may, of course, be the poet himself; he may
be speaking only to himself or to the reader; and there may be no particular
occasion. But frequently the speaker is someone other than the poet, and there
is no more simple-minded mistake in reading poetry than to assume that the
speaker is poet himself simply because he uses the first-person pronoun.
Poems, like short stories, like plays, are fictions. They are sometimes based on
the poet's actual experience, but they need not be, and, even when closest to
actuality, they contain a fictional element. They are works of imagination, not
personal confessions, not transcriptions of personal reality. Their object is
imaginative truth, not fidelity to historical fact.

In Housman's poem the speaker is a shepherd watching his flocks by moon-
light. He is not the poet. His identity is established in the first two lines and con-
firmed in the final stanza. He is talking only to himself (or, more probably,
thinking to himself), for he describes the place as "lonesome" (line 1), and the
sheep graze, he says (in line 2), "beside *me*," not beside *us*. The occasion be-
comes clear in stanzas 4-8: he has a friend in Shrewsbury jail who is to be

hanged in the morning. We can say one thing more about the speaker with some confidence. He is a young shepherd, for he refers to his friend as a "lad" (line 15), and the whole subject of his thinking is the fate of lads like his friend, among whom he numbers himself (line 9).

The physical setting of the poem, like its speaker, is clearly established in the first stanza. It is in the country, on a "moonlit heath" with a rolling terrain, near a crossing of roads (the sheep are grazing on a "lonesome bank" near "four cross ways"). The setting in time is roughly indicated in stanza 3. It is after the Industrial Revolution, for there are railroad trains. Also, the speaker tells us, it is now the custom to hang criminals in the jail. A century earlier, we learn from the last line and the first two stanzas, it was the custom to hang them in the country, by a crossroads, and to leave the bodies hanging there, in chains, as a warning to passers-by. The one possible obscurity in the poem is cleared up by the author's own footnote. He tells us, in a note to the second stanza, that "Hanging in chains was called keeping sheep by moonlight." The body of the hanged man, swinging from the gallows during the night, seemed like a shepherd to be watching over the flocks in the vicinity of the gallows. From these clues we can say that the time of the poem is roughly contemporaneous with its composition, that is, in the closing years of the nineteenth century.

The movement of thought in the poem is clear enough. The speaker, watching over his flocks by moonlight, is reminded by the crossroads that it used to be the custom to hang men there and to leave their bodies hanging in chains. He then reflects that the present custom is to hang men in the city jail and recalls what probably started this train of thought in the first place: that his friend is to be hanged next morning (at 8 A.M., the traditional time for English hangings) in Shrewsbury jail. He concludes by wishing his friend "as sound a sleep" as that of lads who were hanged a century earlier by the crossroads.

The questions we have so far asked, however, do not take us very far. More important is the question, What is the tone of the poem? What is its emotional coloring? What, in other words, is the speaker's attitude toward his friend who is to be hanged? And what is the poet's attitude toward human life?—I have purposely spoken here in one breath of the speaker's attitude and the poet's, for though the speaker is not the poet (the speaker is a young Shropshire shepherd, and Housman was a middle-aged poet from Worcestershire), the *attitudes* of the speaker and the poet coalesce. Emotionally the shepherd speaks for the poet, or for one side of the poet.—Why can we say this? First, because there is no particular attempt to characterize the speaker, to provide him with a sharply realized and separate personality out of which his opinions and attitudes grow. Second, because there is no trace of dramatic irony in the poem. The speaker is not made to contradict himself, or to speak with obvious inappropriateness to the situation, or to act in a way that belies his words. He says and does nothing to put us on our guard against accepting what he says. Rather, we tend to identify with him, and we do so because the poet has identified with him. If we need further evidence, we can get it by reading Housman's other poems, for the attitude expressed here is frequently repeated there. What is that attitude?

It is expressed first of all in the word "careless" (line 5). Since the speaker does not know specifically what offense was committed by this "careless shepherd" long ago, it is significant that he calls him "careless" rather than "criminal." The implication is that he just "got into trouble," not that he did evil. He was the victim of ill luck, not of bad character, evil intention, or original sin. This impression is reinforced by stanza 4, where the speaker says that his friend in Shrewsbury jail was "A better lad, if things went right, / Than most that sleep outside." It was "things" that went wrong for the lad, not *he* that went wrong. The implication that worse lads sleep peacefully outside the jail emphasizes that the universe is run largely by luck or accident, not by the principle of justice. The speaker's friend was "as straight a chap" as "treads upon the land," and he was not unique in his bad luck, for his fate is identified with the fate of lads that "shepherded the moonlit sheep" (hung in chains, that is) "a hundred years ago." The double time reference of the poem—the comparison of the present lad's death in Shrewsbury jail with that of former lads "by the four cross ways" —functions wholly for this purpose: to show that the fate of the present lad is typical. Lads with good hearts and good intentions have been getting into trouble since time began. Housman pictures a universe, then, in which luck or chance is the governing force, not one which is run by a beneficent deity. The phrase, "A neck God made for other use / Than strangling in a string" does not indicate belief in God, but only a defeat of human hope and potential. If it were really God being referred to, He could only be an unjust god, or one powerless to effect His purposes, for He presides over a universe where things do not go right and "straight" lads come to bad ends. The poet's attitude toward man, then, is one of tolerance of his frailties and of compassion for his misfortunes. The speaker, thinking of his friend, recognizes that "There but for the grace of God go I": if things had gone slightly differently, he might himself have been in jail instead of his friend. There is no blame, therefore, for either his friend or the "careless shepherd" of a century before. The most significant line in the poem, for this point of view, is line 9: "They hang us now in Shrewsbury jail." *Not* "We hang them now in Shrewsbury jail." The speaker identifies himself with his unfortunate friend and with all lads who get into trouble, not with a righteous society punishing criminals. By doing so, he makes the lot of his friend and of the "careless shepherd" representative of the lot of all young men.—To understand this is to understand the tone of the poem.

But now, other aspects of the poem demand our attention. Let us begin with the words, for it is with them that the poem starts. A poet chooses his words with one thing in mind: to convey the greatest amount of meaning in the smallest amount of space. To do this he must choose words that are multivalued, that do more than one thing at once. They will not only state but suggest; they will not only convey an objective meaning but also direct emotional response; sometimes they will convey two objective meanings at once.

Why, for instance, does Housman use the word "lad" in lines 15 and 30, instead of "guy" or "fellow"? First, because, "lad" implies youth, as "guy" and "fellow" do not, but, second, because it is a friendly word: it predisposes us to view its referent sympathetically. "Chap" (in line 23) is also a friendly word. "Guy" and "fellow" are less affectionate and are morally neutral. We can speak of "good guys and bad guys" or say that someone is a "mean fellow"; it is difficult to think of a "lad" or a "chap" as being bad or mean.

Then look at the word "straight" in line 23. Housman has strategically placed it so as to bring out two objective meanings. Because it follows the phrases "will stand" and "Heels that held up," it has the physical meaning of "erect" or "straight-backed." But because we have been told, two stanzas before, that this was "A better lad . . . Than most that sleep outside," the word has even more strongly the moral meaning of "honest, trustworthy, straightforward."

Next, look at the word "string" in line 20. Ordinarily we should expect a man to be hanged by a "rope." But the word "string" accentuates the inappropriateness of the fate sustained by "A neck God made for other use." To strangle in a string seems ignominious indeed.

But what does Housman do with language earlier in this stanza that is even more remarkable? He works a pun on the word "ring" together with a grammatical telescoping that enables him to say twice as much as he otherwise could do, in half the number of words. At 8 A. M. the clocks will *r-i-n-g*, and the noose of the hangman will *w-r-i-n-g* the neck of the condemned man. Spelled *r-i-n-g* the verb is intransitive and has "clocks" as its subject. Spelled *w-r-i-n-g* the verb is transitive and takes "neck" as its direct object. By telescoping both the grammatical process and the meanings of these two words, Housman goes immediately from the initial signal, the ringing, to its final result, the hanging, making an imaginative leap across all intervening action. Puns are usually thought of as a device for humor, but Housman uses this pun quite seriously for economy, as a means of gaining greater compression and therefore greater force.

Poets have always done this. Their business is to make words function in more than one way at once, to wring the greatest possible meaning from every word. Is there a suggestion of a pun, too, in the phrase "morning clocks" (line 18), suggesting clocks that are *m-o-u-r-n-i-n-g* for the coming death as well as ringing in the morning? I raise the question to let you answer it as you will.

Next, let us look at the imagery of the poem. By imagery I mean the representation in language of sense experience. Imagery is that quality in a poem which enables us imaginatively to see, hear, smell, taste, or feel the experience presented. Three kinds of imagery predominate in Housman's poem. There is the visual imagery of the moonlit heath, the sheep, and the hanged man standing on air. There is the auditory imagery of chains clanking, whistles blowing, trains groaning, clocks ringing. And there is what may be called the kinesthetic imagery—the sensation of the throat strangling, the neck snapping.

The visual imagery is dominated by the moonlight. That moonlight is kept steadily before us. It is mentioned in the opening line, is returned to in the second stanza where the "careless shepherd" is seen keeping his "flocks by moonlight" with the "glimmering sheep" grazing beneath his hanging body. Both moonlight and sheep return in the closing lines of the poem, so that the whole poem is bathed and framed in moonlight. What is the function of the moonlight? It serves, I think, to soften the emotional focus, to contribute to the pathos, to cast a delicate melancholy over the situation appropriate to the tone.

Sounds are important in this poem, as they are likely to be when one is alone at night. Auditory imagery is thus as important as visual. Housman conveys the quality of the sounds partly by the use of onomatopoeia, the use of words whose sound is an imitation of their meaning. Actually, there are only four onomatopoetic words in the poem, "clank," "groan," "ring," and "snap"—but Housman intensifies their effect by placing them in strategic positions and by repeating their sounds in other words.

The first onomatopoetic word is "clank" at the end of line 3. It intrudes into the quiet beauty of the moonlit scene with a harshness appropriate to the gallows, and thus effectively introduces the discordant note in the speaker's thoughts. It is given unusual emphasis by being made a rhyme word and by being placed at the end of the line—an emphatic position. It reminds us that the bodies left hanging from the gallows were in chains.

The next onomatopoetic word is "groan" in line 11. What makes this word peculiarly effective is the way its final "n" sound is anticipated by the "n's" in "forlorn" and "trains" and echoed by the "n's" in "men" and "morn," and how its long "o" sound is anticipated by the "o" in "blow" and also caught up by the "o's" in the rhyme words "forlorn" and "morn." Thus, these sounds—the sounds of trains passing in the night and of their whistles blowing—seem to echo throughout the stanza.

> The whistles blow forlorn,
> And trains all night groan on the rail
> To men that die at morn.

What is the importance of these sounds? Why does the poet mention them? First, because the sound of a train at night is one of the loneliest sounds in creation. More important, because they tell us something about the lad in

Shrewsbury jail. On the night before his hanging, that lad is awake all night. He hears every sound that passes in the night—every train that slides by, every whistle that blows. In addition, these details place Shrewsbury jail in its modern urban setting, contrasting it with the silent country settings of a century before. The imagery here thus serves a multiple purpose: besides reinforcing the mood and the tone of the poem, it tells us about the state of the lad in jail, and it brings before us the fact of change. But though the externals of life change, it reminds us, the fate of man remains the same. Despite railroads, technological progress, and urbanization, Shropshire lads are getting into trouble and ending up on the gallows just as they have always done.

The third onomatopoetic word is the word "ring" in line 18. Its sound is faintly anticipated earlier in the line by "morning," is emphasized by its position at the end of the line, and is reinforced two lines further on by the rhyming word "string." We have already noted its importance.

The final onomatopoetic word is "snap" in stanza five, and here again we see how the skillful poet, to gain an onomatopoetic effect, does something more than merely use an onomatopoetic word. Housman makes the most of the sound of that word in several ways. It is emphasized by being placed at the end of the line, before a comma; it is reinforced by its collocation with the words "sharp" and "up" and the rhyme word "chap," all of which pick up that snappish final "p." Less obviously, but equally effectively, all the principal words in this stanza are monosyllables, and most of them end with explosive consonants. *Sharp-link-snap-dead-stand-held-straight-chaps-treads-land,* and *life-air-heels*—the very sharpness and abruptness of these short, sharp words in steady procession contributes to the abruptness with which the link of life is snapped.

In talking about the auditory imagery of the poem, we have imperceptibly glided into the kinesthetic imagery, for the snapping of the link of life is not only heard but felt. The most remarkable kinesthetic image, however, is the image of "strangling in a string" in line 20; it is made remarkable by Housman's brilliant maneuvering of sounds. The heavy alliteration of the "str's" in the two principal words of the line, followed by the forceful consonance of the "ng's," emphasizes the fact that in both these words a single short vowel is surrounded and overpowered by five strong consonants, as if they were trying to choke the life out of it. We need very little imagination to feel the struggle of the victim as he gasps for breath in the grip of the noose.

From imagery it is an easy step to figurative language. At least three metaphors contribute to the meanings of the poem. The first is that which compares a corpse hanging in chains to a shepherd keeping his flocks by moonlight. The "careless shepherd" who makes his appearance in stanza 2 and reappears in the final stanza was not, of course, necessarily a shepherd. He may have been a farmer, a carpenter, or tinker; but, after he was hanged, his blank eyes seemed to be gazing out in watchfulness over the sheep.

Next is the "link of life" in line 21. Literally, the word "link" means a connecting loop in a chain, but here its meanings are metaphorical. The "link of life" is that subtle bond that binds body and spirit together; when it is snapped, an inert body remains. But what literally is snapped in the poem is the neck, the link between the head and the trunk. The collocation of "link" with "snap" thus brings out two meanings for both words: "snap" means both to make a snapping sound, and to break; "link" means both the bond between body and spirit, and the neck. The duality of meaning here is the result of metaphor and of strategic arrangement.

Last is the word "sleep." In stanza 4 the word is used quite literally for what we all do every night. In the final stanza, however, it is used by the speaker after he has imagined his friend as having been hanged. He is thus referring to the sleep of death, and is wishing that his friend after death may know a peace that he did not know during life. But he is not only *wishing*, in effect he is *promising* his friend a sound sleep. For the speaker does not believe in immortality or hell. The lads that "shepherded the moonlit sheep / A hundred years ago"—who ended their lives like his friend on the gallows—are not suffering eternal torment in hell; they are sleeping soundly, he believes, as his friend will.

We have already seen how effectively Housman uses the *sounds* of language in this poem. What I wish to emphasize is that, in good poetry, sound is not simply a decorative ornament, like a pair of earrings; it is part of the very expression of the face, a medium of meaning. The poet, that is to say, transmits meaning through the sounds of his words as well as through their denotations. Onomatopoetic words are an obvious example, but the principle operates also in more subtle ways. In line 29, when Housman alliterates the "s's" in "sound" and "sleep," he is not merely pleasing the ear, he is binding together an adjective with the noun it modifies. In line 25, when he alliterates the "w's" in "So here I'll watch the night and wait," he is underlining the grammatical parallelism of the verbs, both predicates of the same subject. In stanza 6, when he slips in the internal rhyme of "dead" and "treads," he is underscoring the contrast between the dead and the quick—those who stand on the air and those who tread on the land. Again, in stanza 5, the alliterating "n's" of "naked," "noose," and "neck" tie together in sound three words that the hanging will bring together in meaning, while the repeated "k's" of "clocks" and "neck" bring into conjunction two things that the sentence structure also joins—the subject and object of the punning verb "rings."

The principle that holds for the sounds of good poetry holds also for its rhythms. The importance of meter is not that it provides a pleasant melody for the words to jig to. Its importance is that it too expresses meaning. A good poet may imitate in the movement of his line the movement of an action being described. Always he uses meter to pick out and emphasize words that are important to his meaning. One great advantage of metrical pattern over free verse is that variations from the pattern become significant.

Housman's basic pattern is one that alternates four iambic feet in the first and third lines of each stanza with three feet in the second and fourth. The pattern, most regular in stanza 7, goes like this:

So HERE / I'll WATCH / the NIGHT / and WAIT /
To SEE / the MORN- / ing SHINE, /
When HE / will HEAR / the STROKE / of EIGHT /
And NOT / the STROKE / of NINE. /

But Housman departs from this strict pattern several times. In line 4, instead of the iambic procession we have been led to expect from the first three lines, he substitutes a trochee in the first foot and a spondee in the last. That is, instead of "Fast BY / the FOUR / cross WAYS, /" we must scan the line "FAST by / the FOUR / CROSS WAYS. /" The result is to force unusual emphasis on "fast" and "cross," and to bring out additional meanings for these words. The phrase "fast by" means "close by" or "near": a meaning now archaic but appropriate to the obsolete location of the gallows. But because the inversion of accent divides the word "fast" from "by" (we must read the phrase "Fast / by the four . . ."), we tend to read a second meaning into the word, that of "firm" or "steadfast." The gallows stood firm by the crossways then, as it does in Shrewsbury jail today. Two meanings for the price of one. In the case of "cross," my argument is more tenuous, and I will not press it, but the word "cross" contains a whisper of "angry," in reference to a society which hangs its offenders, and it may suggest also a symbolical connection between *the* cross and the gallows, in reference to the victim who is hanged, or crucified by society.

Housman departs from his regular pattern again in line 11 by substituting a spondee in the second foot and a trochee in the third:

And TRAINS / ALL NIGHT / GROAN on / the RAIL

These departures work in two ways. The line is drastically slowed down by the cluster of four accented syllables following each other, and unusual emphasis is thrown on the words "all" and "groan." The slowness of the line conforms to the slowness with which the night passes for the sleepless lad. The emphasis on "all" points up his sleeplessness: he does not sleep a wink all night. The emphasis on "groan" intensifies the onomatopoetic sound of the word (the other three onomatopoetic words in the poem all come at the ends of lines) and makes it express the *feelings* of the condemned man as well as the *sound* of the train on the track.

Housman's final departure from his pattern is in line 23. Here a trochaic inversion in the first foot isolates a spondee in the second:

HEELS that / HELD UP / as STRAIGHT / a CHAP /

The result is that the two words "held up" are thrust up, or held up, in the line, just as the chap being spoken of is held up on his heels.

Much more can be said about this poem. There is the effective way that Housman gives it shape and coherence by repeating certain words, phrases, and images. We have seen how he frames the poem with the images of moonlight and sheep in the first and final stanzas. There is also the effective figurative expression by which the man hanging from the gallows seems to be standing on air, a figure which Housman introduces in the second stanza and repeats in the sixth, thus binding those two stanzas together. There is the repeated notion that the man hanging in chains by the crossroads is keeping his sheep by moonlight, a notion introduced in the second stanza and repeated in the last. There is the understated but striking expression for the condemned lad's death in stanza 7, where "he will hear the stroke of eight / And not the stroke of nine"—a turn of speech which catches up the image of the "morning clocks" in stanza 5. There is the effective repetition of words like "lad" and "sleep," both used twice in the poem, in the fourth stanza and the last, thus binding these two stanzas together. Everything, in fact, comes to rest in the final stanza—sleep, moonlight, sheep, the friend in Shrewsbury jail, the speaker, and the lads that hanged in chains a hundred years ago. The final stanza ties up all the threads of the poem.

Reading <u>Miniver Cheevy</u>

The great virtue of the critical movement of the last few decades is that it has taught us to read poems closely and attentively. Its danger is that it sometimes makes the poem seem to exist for the sake of the criticism rather than the criticism for the sake of the poem. I make this observation in an attempt to disarm my reader, for I am about to analyze a poem which he may not consider in need of elucidation. Edwin Arlington Robinson's *Miniver Cheevy* has been popular with both public and critics, and has not been accused of obscurity. But partially for that very reason *Miniver Cheevy* is an excellent poem for demonstrating how poetry "works"; how the poet, by his peculiar juxtaposition of words, by his employment of connotation and figurative language, and by his management of sound, meter, structure, and stanza pattern, adds extra dimensions of meaning and suggests more than he states. Ezra Pound has described poetry as language charged with meaning. An intensive reading of *Miniver Cheevy* will show how the poet gives his words their charge. It will also serve to deepen some tones in Robinson's portrait.

Miniver Cheevy, child of scorn,
  Grew lean while he assailed the seasons;
He wept that he was ever born,
  And he had reasons.

Miniver loved the days of old
  When swords were bright and steeds were prancing;
The vision of a warrior bold
  Would set him dancing.

Miniver sighed for what was not,
  And dreamed, and rested from his labors;
He dreamed of Thebes and Camelot,
  And Priam's neighbors.

Miniver mourned the ripe renown
  That made so many a name so fragrant;
He mourned Romance, now on the town,
  And Art, a vagrant.

Miniver loved the Medici,
  Albeit he had never seen one;

He would have sinned incessantly
    Could he have been one.

Miniver cursed the commonplace
    And eyed a khaki suit with loathing;
He missed the medieval grace
    Of iron clothing.

Miniver scorned the gold he sought,
    But sore annoyed was he without it;
Miniver thought, and thought, and thought,
    And thought about it.

Miniver Cheevy, born too late,
    Scratched his head and kept on thinking;
Miniver coughed, and called it fate,
    And kept on drinking.

The main features of the poem are immediately apparent. Here is the portrait of a misfit, a failure. Unable to adjust himself to the present and meet the problems of reality, he escapes this reality in two ways: first, by dreaming of the romantic past which he has read about in story books, poetry, and history; and second, by drinking. The past seems romantic to him because it is not the present. Miniver is the kind of person who is always longing for "the good old days" and who thinks the present cheap and commonplace, unromantic and unexciting.

Miniver Cheevy, child of scorn,
    Grew lean while he assailed the seasons;
He wept that he was ever born,
    And he had reasons.

"Miniver Cheevy, child of scorn." The first phrase to greet us in the poem is deliberately ambiguous. It means, first, that Miniver, like some of the heroes of whom he reads, has a mythological paternity. His father was Scorn personified, and Miniver is of the first generation, inheriting the attributes of his father. He scorns everything connected with the present: its art, its warfare, its society. He scorns gold, and the materialistic aims of men who seek money rather than glory. And he scorns labor. But the phrase also means that Miniver was the *object* of scorn, as a child of misfortune is one whom misfortunes happen *to*. Miniver receives scorn as well as gives it. He is "at outs" with society, but is also *outcast* from it. And here already we begin to suspect that Miniver's scorn of society is simply a rationalization of his failure to be accepted by it. Henry Thoreau was "at outs" with society and voluntarily withdrew from it for two years at Walden Pond. But Miniver's isolation is not voluntary, and he withdraws, we infer, only as far as the corner table of a city café. There is something superficial about his contempt for the present. The word "child" contributes to this meaning by suggesting his essential immaturity.

Is this ambiguity intentional or simply the product of a reader's ingenuity? If we had to choose between the two readings we should choose the first, for we are told in so many words that Miniver "scorned . . . gold," and in the next line that he "assailed the seasons," and throughout the poem that he "cursed" the modern and the commonplace. Nowhere else are we told explicitly that he was in addition the object of scorn. But unless we are not also to take this interpretation, why did not Robinson capitalize Scorn—as he has done with the personifications of Romance and Art later in the poem?

"Assailed the seasons" is a peculiar phrase. Ordinarily we should say of a man that he "railed at the times." But "seasons" is a figurative equivalent for "times" that has a peculiar value. The rotation of the seasons suggests the persistence in time of Miniver's detraction—spring, summer, fall, winter, year in, year out—in a way that the more common phrase does not. And when "seasons" is combined with "assailed," the four recurring "s" sounds give us the very hiss of Miniver's attacks.

Miniver "grew lean," the context suggests, because of his discontent. We think of the traditional contrast between the lean nagging type and the fat jolly type. We remember that the discontented Cassius had "a lean and hungry look." But "grew lean" also looks forward to later information in the poem. Miniver rests from his labors; he has no money; he drinks. Unlike that of Cassius, Miniver's hunger is physical as well as spiritual. And again is not the relationship reciprocal —Miniver's leanness being not only a result but a cause of his discontent?

The concluding line of the first stanza is, of course, ironical understatement. The absence of a qualifying adjective actually serves to intensify the effect of the line, to multiply Miniver's "reasons." It leaves the effect as of something not all said.

> Miniver loved the days of old
>   When swords were bright and steeds were prancing;
> The vision of a warrior bold
>   Would set him dancing.

"Days of old," "swords . . . bright," "steeds . . . prancing," "warrior . . . bold": This is trite language, but not trite writing. For the triteness is appropriate here. It suggests the superficiality of Miniver's idealization of the past, an idealization based not on an intimate personal knowledge of the past but on hand-me-down sentiments. The phraseology also suggests the source of these sentiments: romantic history and literature. Miniver would be right at home with the current vogue for historical fiction. "Steeds" and "warrior" are romantically connotative words. Substitute "horses" and "soldier" and a certain poetic patina is lost. But in this context the effect of this romantic connotation is ironical: it suggests not a real but a false patina. It suggests that Miniver's love of the past inheres in words rather than in reality. "The vision of a warrior bold/Would set him dancing" may be interpreted literally or metaphorically. We may imagine that if Miniver ever really saw a medieval knight, he would arise and do a little jig of pleasure. The imaginary vision—the picture in the mind's eye—sets his soul dancing.

> Miniver sighed for what was not,
>   And dreamed, and rested from his labors;
> He dreamed of Thebes and Camelot,
>   And Priam's neighbors.

Miniver "rested from his labors." This is ironical understatement. Read literally, it would mean that he took a short time out from hard work to recuperate his strength before returning to work again. In context it means that he desisted from labors that were probably almost non-existent in the first place. The effect of pluralizing "labor"—ordinarily we should expect the singular—is twofold. It exaggerates the irony by increasing the "labor" that Miniver desisted from. One thinks, perhaps, of the labors of Hercules. But it also suggests a certain discontinuity in the labor that Miniver actually rested from. We may presume that Miniver never held one job long.

The allusions to Thebes, Camelot, and Troy again indicate the source of Miniver's love of the past, for all three cities are centers of rich lengendary cycles. Priam's "neighbors" included, of course, Hector, Helen, Paris, Cassandra, Laocoön, Troilus and Criseyde, and, by implication, Achilles, Ajax, Ulysses, Agamemnon, and all the rest. The effect of introducing the homely word "neighbors" into this context is ludicrous; and the ludicrousness reacts not on Troy but on Miniver. There were, of course, two ancient cities named Thebes, both famous, one in Greece, one in Egypt. The primary reference is to the city in Greece. Founded by Cadmus, its walls built to music by Amphion, the birthplace of Dionysius and Hercules, it achieves its greatest fame as the scene of the stories centering around Oedipus and Antigone. But the Egyptian Thebes is equally famous, is mentioned in Homer, and is noted for its majestic temples. The effect of the ambiguity is to enrich the reference, and to make it hold good for a reader familiar with either Thebes more than the other.

> Miniver mourned the ripe renown
>   That made so many a name so fragrant;
> He mourned Romance, now on the town,
>   And Art, a vagrant.

"Ripe" is not the adjective we expect to be coupled with "renown." Thus juxtaposed, the two words interact, each giving the other a slight pejorative twist in connotation. "Renown" gets a twist in the direction of "notoriety": the suggestion is of something juicy, too-much-talked-of; "ripe renown" is not the same as "great renown." "Ripe" concurrently loses the entirely favorable connotation that it has when used with words like "wisdom" and "age" and is twisted in the direction of "over-ripe." "Fragrance" is even more affected by this context. Ordinarily it might suggest springtime and blossoms; with "ripe" in the context it suggests fall and decayed fruit. Obviously Robinson is preparing for his conjunction in the next stanza of Medici and sin, the Medici being more notorious than glorious. But the influence also acts backward to remind us that Troy, Camelot, and Thebes mean not only Hector, Galahad, and Antigone, but Helen, Guinevere, and Jocasta—a harlot, an adulteress, and a woman who married her own son. Miniver is interested not only in bright costumes, heroic deeds, and feats of arms, but also in love affairs not always legitimate.

Romance and Art are personified, and both are down in their fortunes. The collocation of the eloquent word "Romance" with the slang phrase "on the town" emphasizes the shabby company the former finds herself in. It also suggests a cause. "Town" in this context really means "city," and the disappearance of romance for Miniver parallels the growth of modern metropolitan civilization. Literally the phrase means "engaged in prostitution" or "living off organized charity." Romance can eke out an existence today only by selling herself or accepting such hand-outs as the city will give her. Art is a tramp; that is, not only a shabby beggar but a wanderer—someone who has gone away.

> Miniver loved the Medici,
>   Albeit he had never seen one;
> He would have sinned incessantly
>   Could he have been one.

"Miniver loved the Medici." The alliteration and metrical similarity of the two nouns links them together in sound as well as in thought. The placing of the Medici between references to Art and to sin is as strategic as was the placing of "ripe renown" between Troy and the Medici, for the Medici were patrons of one as they were perpetrators of the other. Miniver "would have sinned incessantly." Again the hissing "s" sounds reinforce the meaning, lending an evil undertone and perhaps suggesting the repetition of act proposed and Miniver's glee in the prospect. The false rhyme ("seen one-been one") furnishes an echo of the false note in Miniver's romantic imagination.

> Miniver cursed the commonplace
>   And eyed a khaki suit with loathing;
> He missed the medieval grace
>   Of iron clothing.

Alliteration again operates powerfully in the next stanza, linking "cursed," "commonplace," and "khaki" together in one unit of meaning, and "missed" and "medieval" in another. But the main effect of the stanza is its irony, the word "grace" standing for its opposite, "metallic rigidity." The irony is established by the ludicrous substitution of "iron clothing" for "armor." "Grace of armor" might pass muster; "grace of iron clothing" brings out a clank. The irony is functional, for it again suggests the superficiality of Miniver's medieval idealization. Miniver saw the grace, missed the clank, had obviously never read the chapter in which Mark Twain's Connecticut Yankee gets a fly inside his helmet. The superficiality is doubly emphasized by the fact that for Miniver romance inheres in clothes, themselves a superficial thing.

> Miniver scorned the gold he sought,
>   But sore annoyed was he without it;
> Miniver thought, and thought, and thought,
>   And thought about it.

"Miniver scorned the gold he sought." Does the paradox in Miniver's behavior represent an unconscious ambivalence of values or merely a conscious bowing to the hard facts of living? Thoreau denounced materialism but knew that a man must earn his bread, and he made provision for it in his scheme of life. Miniver's scorn is rationalization of the fact that his seeking has been unsuccessful. We know this from his selective use of literature and history. The heroes of Thebes, Camelot, and Troy were upper class people with plenty of wealth, who killed each other for love, not money. And are not the Medici even more famous for money than for sin? They could sin so gloriously precisely because of this money. If Miniver could have been any character in history, he would have chosen to be of the richest family of all. That Miniver "thought, and thought, and thought, and thought about it" reinforces the suggestion.

Robert Frost has recorded his delight at the placing of the fourth "thought" in this stanza. "There is more to it than the number of 'thoughts'. There is the way the last one turns up by surprise around the corner, the way the shape of the stanza is played with, the easy way the obstacle of verse is turned to advantage." The last "thought," of course, is the drop that overflows the bucket. It emphasizes the futility of Miniver's thinking, which gets nowhere, as the repetition emphasizes its repetitiveness.

> Miniver Cheevy, born too late,
>   Scratched his head and kept on thinking;
> Miniver coughed, and called it fate,
>   And kept on drinking.

"Born too late" has ironical implications, for the reader knows by now that Miniver would have been the same in any era. It is his inability to cope with present reality that is Miniver's curse, and this curse is an accident of character, not history. But Miniver calls it "fate," rationalizing to the end, externalizing the blame, not realizing that character is fate. "Miniver coughed"—he has been drinking too much and eating too little—"And kept on drinking." The alliteration of the key verbs—"kept," "coughed," "called," "kept"—and the feminine rhymes underline the continuance of the activity. The last line is a vivid stroke of poetic economy. We have not been told before that Miniver has been drinking. Usually we are told that someone has been doing something before we are told that he "kept on" doing it. But Robinson omits the former, and still makes us feel that we have known this all along. He prepares us with "coughed," and then with the parallelism of "kept on drinking" with "kept on thinking" causes the reader to supply a "drank, and drank, and drank, and drank" to match the previous repetition of "thought."

So much for the internal structure of the poem. Of the stanza form Ellsworth Barnard, in his able analysis of Robinson's technique, has pointed out the felicity: "The short last line with its feminine ending provides precisely the anticlimax that is appropriate to the ironic contrast between Miniver's gilded dream and the tarnished actuality." He also comments on the submerged refrain in the use of Miniver's full name at the beginning of the first and last stanzas and his first name at the beginning of the others. This refrain keeps both the character and his name constantly before us.

And what of the name? It is perhaps the most unusual one in all of Robinson. It sounds a little silly, and certainly out of place in our world, as Miniver himself is. But there are other reasons that may have suggested it. "Miniver," according to Webster's Second Edition, is a "fur esteemed in the Middle Ages as a part of costume (from *menu* small, plus *vair* a kind of fur)." "Cheevy" is not too distant from "chevalier" and "chivalry"—knights and knighthood. Or, if we search the New English Dictionary, we find *chevy*, a "chase, pursuit, hunt" or "hunting cry"; or the obsolete *cheve*—"to do homage to"; or *chevasaile*—"The collar of a coat, gown, or other garment; in the 14th c. often richly ornamented," a word used in *The Romance of the Rose* and more recently by Rossetti. Whichever of these words we link it to, Miniver's name, first and last, represents the kind of things he dreamed about, and links him to the middle ages.*

One consideration remains to be discussed—Miniver's relation to his creator. A reader unfamiliar with Robinson's life and temperament, coming across Hagedorn's assertion that in *Miniver Cheevy* Robinson "spoofed" himself, would and should properly be shocked. Here surely, he would say, if ever there was one, is an objective poem. But the more we know of Robinson, the more plausible Hagedorn's suggestion becomes. The objectivity lies in Robinson's ability to look at himself with humor, to externalize one side of himself.

---

*I am indebted for the above suggestions to a former colleague, James Rushing.

Three aspects of Robinson's life and character are embodied in Miniver Cheevy:

1. All his life Robinson denounced the materialistic standards of his age. In poems like "Cassandra" we hear Robinson himself, under the thinnest of disguises, "assailing the seasons" and "scorning the gold." Robinson judged and condemned the materialistic standards of success and failure in Tilbury Town (whose god was the till). But paradoxically Robinson could not keep from judging himself by those same standards. He was haunted by the idea of failure; he worried and tormented himself by seeing himself through his neighbors' eyes as a misfit and dreamer who rested from his labors. There was thus a real ambivalence in Robinson's attitudes. He at once rose above but could not completely shake off the standards of his society. He judged others by his own yardstick, but could not forbear measuring himself by society's. He scorned the gold he sought but was sore annoyed without it. And he "thought, and thought, and thought, and thought about it."

2. No less than Miniver did Robinson dream "of Thebes and Camelot, and Priam's neighbors." In *Isaac and Archibald* he records directly and beautifully his early love of the Greek classics, of "ships and sunlight, streets and singing, / Troy falling, and the ages coming back, . . ."

And Agamemnon was a friend of mine;
Ulysses coming home again to shoot
With bows and feathered arrows made another.

In his twenties he translated Sophocles' *Antigone* into English blank verse. His work throughout makes manifest the enduring quality of this love. The love of Malory was also early and eventuated finally in his three long poems *Merlin, Lancelot,* and *Tristram* (which are distinguished, however, by their realistic treatment and the absence of medieval trappings and "iron clothing").

3. And, like Miniver, Robinson fell prey, for a period in his life, to the drink habit; feared, indeed, that it might get the best of him—and it did come close to ruining his talent. But unlike Miniver, Robinson cured himself, though the effort was not easy. The curious reader will find the experience sympathetically related in Hagedorn's biography. In Robinson's poetry it is allegorically treated in *The Dark House* and is undoubtedly made use of in *The Man Who Died Twice.*

In *Miniver Cheevy* Robinson embodied one side of himself, consciously exaggerated, and perceived with a wry ironic humor. But it was one side only, and the very existence of the poem testifies to the vast difference between that one side and the totality. For the poem testifies to the existence of an insight, a self-knowledge, a grip on reality, and a humorous perception, that Miniver utterly lacked. It is this self-knowledge, this humor, this reality, which reveal Robinson's central sanity, and completely and forever separate the creator from his creature.

Interpreting Poetry—
Two Ways of Going Wrong

A printer locking type into a form for the press must first see that all his lines are of the same width; that is, he must have exactly enough type to fill a rectangular area evenly when packed together. If he leaves a hole in the middle of any line, the whole body of type will fall out for lack of pressure to hold it in place. If he tries to squeeze extra type characters into any line, again the whole body of it will fall apart for lack of pressure on the other lines. There must be just enough type to fill up the rectangular space, no more and no less.

In a similar way, an interpretation of a poem, to be valid, must account for all major facts of the poem, omitting none and adding none. If it leaves out of account important facts of the poem, the interpretation falls apart. If it introduces extra facts into the poem—facts that aren't really there—again it falls apart. Unsuccessful readings of poetry usually fail in one of these two ways. Either they distort the poem by getting too little out of it, or else they falsify it by reading meaning into it. Either they export meaning from the poem by ignoring important facts and details, or they import meaning into it by inventing facts and details.

To illustrate the first kind of failure, let us look at a famous poem by Edwin Arlington Robinson:

RICHARD CORY

Whenever Richard Cory went down town,
We people on the pavement looked at him:
He was a gentleman from sole to crown,
Clean favored, and imperially slim.

And he was always quietly arrayed,
And he was always human when he talked;
But still he fluttered pulses when he said,
"Good-morning," and he glittered when he walked.

And he was rich—yes, richer than a king—
And admirably schooled in every grace:
In fine, we thought that he was everything
To make us wish that we were in his place.

So on we worked, and waited for the light,
And went without the meat, and cursed the bread;

And Richard Cory, one calm summer night,
Went home and put a bullet through his head.

Richard Cory is not a difficult poem. It is the work of Robinson which appears most frequently in anthologies. For Robinson it was pretty much what *Valse Triste* must have been for Sibelius: he wished that people might know him for some other poems besides this one. It is far from being his most significant poem. But it is a fine poem and deserves to be anthologized. And it *is* anthologized partly because it seems so easily understood.

Yet how many times have students identified the theme of the poem as this: Great wealth does not guarantee happiness. That Robinson's talent should be so lavishly expended to produce only such a trite truism as this! Not that the poem does not say this, only that it says so much more. This, indeed, is the theme one might choose for the poem if he read *only* lines 9 and 16. It ignores nine-tenths of the poem.

Only one line of the poem tells us that Richard Cory is rich. The rest of the poem is devoted to telling us about his other qualities, and about his relationship to the people in the town. The first two lines indicate that he is the cynosure of all eyes; the first three stanzas tell us why. First, he is a gentleman. A gentleman in what sense? In the old sense of one who is well-born, or in the modern sense of one who is well-behaved and considerate of others? In both. The latter because we are told that he is "admirably schooled in every grace," and because we hear him courteously saying "Good-morning" to the people on the pavement. The former because the word "gentleman" is one of a constellation of words which by their denotations or connotations suggest aristocratic or royal privilege: "crown," "favored," "imperially," "arrayed," "glittered," "king," "grace," "fine." Four of these words suggest high birth by their secondary meanings: "crown" means top of the head, but it is also a symbol of royalty; "clean-favored" means clean-featured, but "favored" is also privileged; "grace" here means social nicety, but it is also the term used for addressing a duke; "in fine" means in sum, but "fine" implies also a quality of character and dress. Richard Cory, then, is well-born and well-behaved. He is also of attractive appearance, "Clean favored, and imperially slim." He has excellent taste, for he is "quietly arrayed": the juxtaposition of these two words (we might have expected "gorgeously arrayed") was a beautiful stroke, for one word suggests splendor and the other its opposite. Together the two words qualify rather than cancel each other. Cory wears the very finest clothes, they tell us, yet is not in the least ostentatious. The phrase "he glittered when he walked" in this context becomes richly suggestive. "Glittered" may hint literally at a gold watch chain, but in the framework of Cory's quiet good taste it applies metaphorically to his whole appearance and bearing—his good looks, his slim figure, his good clothes, and his good bearing as he walks. Cory does not slouch, or lounge, or sidle; he walks upright with grace and dignity. The most important descriptive detail about Cory, however, is that "he was always human when he talked." For all his good birth and good fortune, there is nothing proud or condescending about him; his courtesy is not a cold formality or gesture of *noblesse oblige*; he appears to have genuine interest in the people he talks to, he puts them at their ease at the same time that he flutters their pulses; his attractions are not merely those of appearance, manner, possessions, and taste, they are the attractions of humanity too. The speaker sums it all up when he says,

> In fine, we thought that he was everything
> To make us wish that we were in his place.

"We thought that he *was* everything," notice; not "We thought that he *had* everything." Cory is an enviable creature to the townsfolk not by virtue of what he possesses but by virtue of what he is.

The theme of *Richard Cory*, then, is something much more wide-sweeping than "Wealth does not guarantee happiness"; it is that good birth, good looks, good breeding, good taste, humanity, *and* wealth do not guarantee happiness. Richard Cory had them all; yet he committed suicide.

So, one type of misreading, the type that leaves important parts of the poem out of account—in this case nine-tenths of the poem. To illustrate the second type of misreading, let us turn to a poem by James Joyce:

CHAMBER MUSIC: XXXVI

I hear an army charging upon the land,
    And the thunder of horses plunging, foam about their knees:
Arrogant, in black armor, behind them stand,
    Disdaining the reins, with fluttering whips, the charioteers.

They cry unto the night their battle-name:
    I moan in sleep when I hear afar their whirling laughter.
They cleave the gloom of dreams, a blinding flame,
    Clanging upon the heart as upon an anvil.

They come shaking in triumph their long, green hair:
    They come out of the sea and run shouting by the shore.
My heart, have you no wisdom thus to despair?
    My love, my love, my love, why have you left me alone?

I have given this poem to college classes for interpretation, with rather surprising results. The poem seems to be speaking about death, wrote one student. Just as the charioteers do not guide their horses, but plunge them into the sea, wrote another, so the poet cannot control his emotions, but is plunged into a sea of loneliness. The poet is thrown into despair by the pressures and troubles of the world, wrote three others; he wonders why his love has left him to face these troubles alone. The poet is writing with a reminiscent attitude, wrote a sixth; Joyce is thinking about the movement of the sea which beats onto his homeland, Ireland; he hears the wind across the water as whirling laughter; in the closing lines he presents his sentiments toward his homeland and indicates that he feels deserted.

Each of these misreadings illustrates what happens when the reader imports materials into the poem that aren't in the poem itself. The sixth student's reading illustrates it most clearly. This student, one might almost say, knew too much about James Joyce. He knew that Joyce had strong but mixed feelings toward his homeland. He knew that Joyce felt rejected by his countrymen, and that he left Ireland as a young man and went into exile on the continent. He knew also that Joyce, though he never returned to Ireland, continued to think and write about it for the rest of his life. He imported all of this biographical material into his reading of the poem.

We must assume of a successful poem that it is a self-contained unit, that it contains within itself all the materials necessary for interpretation. This is not to say that the reader must not know the meanings of words or be familiar with the matter referred to by historical or literary allusions. But the words and allusions are in the poem itself, and the reader should not bring in outside knowledge unless the poem itself commands that he do so. Above all, he should not begin by importing the poet into the poem. The poet is the poem's maker, not its subject. A poem is an imaginative construct, not a personal confession. Without good reason to do otherwise, we should think of the speaker in a poem as a fictional person, not the poet himself. In this poem we have no evidence to identify the speaker as James Joyce, nothing to identify the setting as Ireland, nothing to indicate that the poem is a reminiscence: the words are in the present tense; the outcry at the end seems very immediate. What *do* we have in this poem itself?

We have first of all a speaker who "hears," who "moans in sleep," who reproves his heart for despairing, and who asks why his love has left him alone. In addition, we have an extended image of an army of charioteers that charges out of the sea upon the land (not *into* the sea, as the second student wrote). No actual army of charioteers ever came out of the sea, of course, and no literal charioteers ever had long, green hair; so this cannot be a literal army (as several students interpreted it); it must be metaphorical. What *actually* charges out of the sea upon the land? Waves, of course. The waves breaking upon the land, then, are being compared to an army. All the details of the image support this identification. The "thunder" of the "plunging" horses is the thunder of the waves; the comparison of waves to horses has been natural to poetic imagination ever since Neptune was first pictured as driving sea horses; it is more recently found in such lines as Matthew Arnold's "The wild white horses foam and fret." The "foam" about the horses' knees clearly fits into this image, as does the "long, green hair" of the charioteers, suggestive of seaweed. The waves seem driven ashore, as if by charioteers; yet they are unchecked: the charioteers disdain the reins. The "fluttering whips" may suggest the flying spray that beats over the foamy crests of the whitecaps. The shouting, the battle-cries, and the whirling laughter, like the "thunder," suggest the noise and clamor of the waves.

This identification, however, though it explains most of the details of the army-image, does not explain all of them. Why are the charioteers "arrogant," why are they dressed in "black armor," why do they utter "whirling laughter," why do they "shout in triumph?" To answer these questions we must revert to other details of the poem. The speaker has been deserted by his love; he is in despair. The charging army offers, then, not just a visual image but an emotional image. It is the embodiment of the speaker's sorrows, of his despair. It is armored in black in consonance with his gloom; it is arrogant and triumphant and utters whirling laughter, because his hopes have been defeated, because life seems to deride and mock him.

And where *is* the speaker? Since he moans "in sleep," since the charioteers "cleave the gloom of dreams," and since he "hears" the army rather than sees it, he is clearly in bed, sleeping a restless sleep within hearing of the roar of the sea.

The poem itself, then, furnishes all the details necessary to its interpretation. The speaker has been deserted by his love; he is consequently in despair; he would like to be "wise" and to take this disappointment calmly, but his heart has no "wisdom," he cannot; the roar of the breakers reacting upon his desolation gives rise to a half-nightmare, half-waking-fancy of the sea as an army of arrogant charioteers with fluttering whips who laugh in triumph over his defeat. The poem embodies the speaker's despair.

There is no reason to import James Joyce or Ireland into the poem; and we should not do so. If we wish to tie the poem to some personal disappointment in love in Joyce's life, there is nothing to stop us from doing so; but in doing so we should be interpreting Joyce, not the poem. There is certainly no justification for interpreting the poem as about death; only the adjective "black," which can be otherwise explained, even remotely suggests death.

These misreadings are idiosyncratic and easily dismissed. Let me return, however, to one other misreading, since several students fell into it. "The dreamer despairs and wonders why his love left him to face the troubles of the world alone," wrote one. "The nightmare symbolizes all the pressures of life which are exerted upon the individual; the appeal to love as a remedy for the situation affords no escape," wrote another. The common element in these two judgments is that both adduce *two* reasons for the speaker's despair: first, the troubles and pressures of the world; second, his desertion by his love. But is there any reason for adducing more than one? Is not the speaker's desertion itself sufficient to explain his desolation? Again we appeal to the principle that we must import nothing into the poem in order to explain it. Joyce presents us with the *effect* of the speaker's sorrow before he presents us with its *cause*, but this inversion should not conceal from us the cause-effect relationship. The speaker's desolation and his desertion by his love are causally related to each other and need not be related through some third item not indicated by the poem itself. The simplest explanation which accounts for all the facts is always the best one.

The printer locks his type into the form confident that it will not fall out, for he has put into the form just enough type to fill up solidly the prescribed rectangular area. The successful reader of a poem arrives at his interpretation confident that it will hold together, for he has accounted for all its major details and left none out of account. Interpreting a poem is, of course, a much more complex activity than locking type into a form, for the type form is little more than two-dimensional, whereas the poem in its richness of meaning is multidimensional. No interpretation of a poem, therefore, is ever complete, and it is questionable if completeness would be desirable were it possible. But if the reader has been reasonably careful about squaring his interpretation with the facts of the poem, further interpretation will only extend and deepen his reading, it will not prove him wrong.

"But Deliver Us From Evil"

Everyone knows that there has been a revolution in the teaching and in the critical analysis of poetry. We are all profoundly grateful for that revolution. It has taught us to look at *poems* instead of at something else—at the historical background, the social milieu, the biography or personal idiosyncrasies of the poet. Not that these matters are unimportant, but that, in the study of poetry, they belong properly to the background. The poem now occupies the foreground. No longer are poems merely footnotes to some more easily approachable text.

Yet no student of history will be particularly surprised that the revolution has not brought about utopia. No revolution ever has. Changes are made, improvements are effected, but utopia eludes us. Perhaps there is something stubborn in human nature that resists perfection. Or perhaps our improvements in ways of doing things bring their own problems and have their own limitations. The revolution in poetry reading has placed sharp tools in our hands. It has not ensured us skill in handling them.

The title of this paper suggests a sermon, and a sermon demands a text. I take one from T. S. Eliot (*The Frontiers of Criticism*):

> A recent critical method is to take a well-known poem without reference to the author or to his other work, analyse it stanza by stanza and line by line, and extract, squeeze, tease, press every drop of meaning out of it that one can. It might be called the lemon-squeezer school of criticism.

Eliot had recently read a book in which twelve critics applied this method to different poems. His comment was a wry one: "To study twelve poems each analyzed so painstakingly is a very tiring way of passing the time."

Since T. S. Eliot is often regarded as a founding father or early prophet of the "New Criticism," his remarks have unusual interest. Certainly we cannot impute to him the romantic fallacy that to analyze is to destroy. His distress is rather over the lengths to which analysis has been carried. He feels, we might say, as a philosopher of the French Revolution might have felt when contemplating the Reign of Terror. What Eliot contemplates is the reign of tedium. What the revolution has produced is the publication of book after book in which minute analysis is succeeded by minute analysis. To read such books straight through is worse than tiring; it is an exercise in self-inflicted torture. The only possible way to use such books is as reference works. Check the index for the poem one is interested in, and skim the author's analysis. If the book has no index, burn it!

But it is foolish to rail against dullness. And it would be worse than foolish to try to stop incipient critics from attempting to find in a literary work all that is to be found in it, and then publishing their results. We can put up with this, and occasionally be grateful for it. What we cannot be grateful for is the efforts of those who find what is *not* in a literary work, and never was, and publish their results. Not dissemination of dullness, but dissemination of error, is the enemy. For let us admit it. It is possible to get so close to a literary work that one begins to look at it cross-eyed. It is possible to plumb a poem so deeply that one knocks a hole in the bottom and falls through. Unless the critic steps back for a long view from time to time, his vision blurs; the meanings begin to proliferate in every direction. No word but is ambiguous. No phrase but is allusive. No image but is symbolic. No statement but exists at several levels of meaning. In the nightmare of uncontrolled interpretation the bounds of context disappear. Meanings and overtones, like hungry lions, run rampant. Discretion and good sense are gobbled up, and bloody masticated fragments of poem are dribbled everywhere.

The temptation here is to point to horrible examples: an analysis in *College English* here, an analysis in *The CEA Critic* there, an analysis in *The Explicator* yonder, and countless analyses in presumably even more scholarly and learned periodicals. But who knows who may be reading this? Let me illustrate rather with hypothetical examples, to demonstrate the dangers that lie in wait for the over-eager explicator.

First a four-line poem by Amy Lowell:

WIND AND SILVER

Greatly shining
The Autumn moon floats in the thin sky;
And the fish-ponds shake their backs and flash their dragon scales
As she passes over them.

A delicate descriptive poem, the simple-minded reader might say. It presents the image of a beautiful full moon reflected back in a thousand fragments of light from the many-faceted surfaces of fish-ponds as a breeze draws across them. The imaginative effectiveness of the poem springs from its metaphorical likening of fish-ponds to dragons, their breeze-shaken surfaces looking like the scales on a dragon's back. The poem presents an image, the simple-minded reader says, and nothing more.

Blessings on the simple-minded reader! Let him not draw closer. For if he presses his nose up tight against the pane of the poem, what does he see? Dragons! Are not dragons evil? Surely Miss Lowell could not have introduced a dragon into her poem without being aware of the associations and meanings that dragons have gathered around them during the course of centuries! And the moon! Is not the moon traditionally the embodiment of beauty and chastity? Surely the poem has sexual undertones. All of Greek mythology testifies to the rich implications and meanings of the moon for man's imagination. Moreover, does not folklore tell us that the moon drives people mad? The word "lunatic" stands in eloquent testimony to this belief. And then, in the poem, it is night! Is not night associated in our minds with irrational impulse, uncontrolled desire, the id, evil, death? And so we begin to see that this innocent-seeming poem is less innocent than it seems. It packs into its four lines a wealth of implication; it states a deep central truth about the human condition: The forces of evil in nature, symbolized by the dragon in the fish-pond, are set loose at night, when conscious control is relaxed, aroused by the maddening moon, symbol of beauty and chastity, which by its very innocence awakes brutal desire and stirs up the beast in man.

If this poem is not so innocent as it first appeared, it has lost its innocence through being raped by our hypothetical critic. Dragons, the moon, and night all have potentially the meanings ascribed to them, but these meanings are released only when the context provides a triggering mechanism. In Miss Lowell's poem there is no triggering mechanism, and these meanings are simply irrelevant. There is, after all, no dragon in the poem: there is only the moonlight reflected from fish-ponds—an image of beauty, not of terror. The moon in the poem is indeed beautiful, but when we have made this simple declarative statement, we have said all that needs to be said: nothing is gained through elevating the moon to the status of a symbol. Moreover, there is no mythological framework in the poem, necessary to release the suggestion of chastity, an attribute of Diana. As for the night, can we exhibit the moon in all its beauty except at night?

Wordsworth was impatient with Peter Bell because

A primrose by a river's brim
A yellow primrose was to him,
And it was nothing more.

Peter should have seen in the primrose a feast for the eye, a joy to the heart, and a pair of wings for the spirit. But would not Wordsworth have been even more impatient if Peter had seen in it a re-enactment of the burial and resurrection of the god Osiris?

Here is another poem about the moon, this time by Walter de la Mare:

THE HORSEMAN

I heard a horseman
    Ride over the hill;
The moon shone clear,
    The night was still;
His helm was silver,
And pale was he;
And the horse he rode
    Was of ivory.

This poem almost immediately teases one by its suggestiveness. There is, first of all, a "horseman," and the horseman is "pale." Must not the horseman be Death

—the traditional "pale rider"? The possibility is supported by the words "night" and "still." "Night" is a natural symbol of death; and "still" suggests the stillness of death. Thus the words "horseman," "pale," "night," and "still" seem to imply a pattern. Yet, strong as this implication is, it should be resisted. The horseman wears a "helm": is Death ever so depicted? The moon is "clear," not darkened. The horseman carries no reaping-hook, nor even spear or sword. The poem gives no hint that this rider is ominous or threatening or coming after anyone. The narrator is not terrified. There are no dead bodies in the horseman's path. In short, though the associations of these words do add a sense of mystery and awesomeness to the poem, a reading which interprets the poem as being *about* death is insufficiently supported, and even contradicted, by the evidence. Such a reading is suggested by only four words, all of which can be explained, together with other details of the poem, by a simpler interpretation.

De la Mare is fascinated in this poem by the effect on a still clear night of moonlight on a moving figure below. This effect is to make the horseman "pale," his helm "silver," and his horse "ivory." There are contrasts between images of light and darkness, and between sound ("I heard a horseman") and stillness. Only this and little more. The night has its own strangeness, its own eerie beauty, unconnected with death, for the poet who also wrote the often-reprinted *Silver*:

> Slowly, silently, now the moon
> Walks the night in her silver shoon;
> This way, and that, she peers, and sees
> Silver fruit upon silver trees; . . .

The Horseman has the same kind of subject as *Silver*.

To mention de la Mare is to call to mind *The Listeners*—a celebrated case in point. Even more than *The Horseman* it tempts the reader into symbolic interpretations. By various readers the Traveller who knocks on the moonlit door has been identified with "God, Christ, the Holy Ghost, *a* ghost, Man, *a* man, or Walter de la Mare"; and the listeners have been made to stand for "the powers of darkness, the riddle of life, the dead, a living household, Man, or de la Mare's schoolmates." These interpretations have, I hope, been forever knocked on the head by Frederick L. Gwynn and Ralph W. Condee in an excellent discussion in *The Explicator* (February 1954). As Gwynn and Condee convincingly demonstrate, de la Mare's concern here is with conveying an *impression*—an impression of emptiness and silence—and he succeeds so well that the emptiness becomes almost tangible and the silence audible (it "answers" the Traveller's cry and "surges softly backward" when he is gone). *The Listeners* is a poem of the order of *Wind and Silver* and *The Horseman*: almost magical in its effectiveness, but innocent of allegorical meanings.

It is relatively easy to discover sin in the close readings of others; it is harder to guard against it in one's own. Vanity prompts us, once we attempt a close reading, to find as much in a work as possible. Nothing is quite so heady as the feeling that one has discovered in a poem some meaning or beauty that no one else has previously seen there. And so, once we commit ourselves to finding as much as possible, we almost inevitably find more than is legitimate. The very sharpness of our critical tools tends to bring out the weaknesses in our character. We are like foolish teen-agers behind the wheels of powerful automobiles. The temptation to show how clever we are is irresistible.

The burden of my sermon, then, is this: in close reading, prudence is a greater virtue than daring, tact than ingenuity. If a choice must be made, the over-simple interpretation is preferable to the over-subtle, the over-ingenuous to the over-ingenious. As Richard Wilbur writes in an essay which is itself a model demonstration of sensitivity and tact in close reading (*Round About a Poem of Housman's*): "Readers and critics must be careful not to be cleverer than necessary; and there is no greater obtuseness than to treat all poets as Metaphysicals, and to insist on discovering puns which are not likely to be there." The close reader's daily prayer should be, "Lord, keep me humble. Please, let not my light be blinding." In the interpretation of poetry "a little learning" is still "a dangerous thing," and greater learning may be even more dangerous, unless it is balanced by judgment, good sense, and tact.

Though this paper has pretended to be about the close reading of literature, the more theologically-minded of my readers will recognize that it is really about original sin. My targets have been vanity, ambition, pride, and absence of self-restraint. Unfortunately, a prime characteristic of original sin is that it is something of which we *all* are guilty. Some things I have said have made my own ears burn. Indeed, if I have been able to discourse feelingly on sin and temptation it is because I myself have known temptation—and have succumbed to it. I hope that I may be forgiven for these sins. But I refuse to forgive the same sins in others.

Part Two

The Poem
in Relation
to Other Poems

A question too often asked by teachers (and critics) of poetry is the question "Is this a good poem?" or, alternatively, "Is this a bad poem?" The student is left floundering, wondering what he can say. He is presented, say, with the poem *Trees* by Joyce Kilmer, and is *wanted* to identify it as a bad poem, though his disposition is to like it. The trouble with such a question is the implicit assumption it makes that all poetry can be divided into two categories—good and bad— and that every poem has its appropriate label. There are, in fact, infinite gradations of merit (*Trees* doesn't belong at the bottom of the heap), and no reader should be asked to make a judgment without being given a standard of comparison. The only meaningful question is "Which of these two poems is better?" or "Which of these several poems is best?—followed always by a second question, "Why?"

The following group of essays consists of exercises in comparative evaluation. In each case two poems are presented—unidentified by author, or both by the same author—and a judgment between them is called for. The essay suggests how the exercise might be answered. These exercises call for coarse discriminations, not fine discriminations. Literary judgment is not an exact science, and it seems better here to choose examples in which a critical consensus could be easily obtained. For a student, moreover, there is profitable exercise in knocking over straw men. In fact, for the student, the main problem may be in learning to recognize straw. As a teacher, some of my most rewarding experiences have come when students have told me they changed their minds while working on such an exercise, switching their allegiance from the poorer to the better poem. One knows, then, that the learning process is taking place.

Two Poems on Spring

A PRAYER IN SPRING

Oh, give us pleasure in the flowers today;
And give us not to think so far away
As the uncertain harvest; keep us here
All simply in the springing of the year.

Oh, give us pleasure in the orchard white,
Like nothing else by day, like ghosts by night;
And make us happy in the happy bees,
The swarm dilating round the perfect trees.

And make us happy in the darting bird
That suddenly above the bees is heard,
The meteor that thrusts in with needle bill,
And off a blossom in mid air stands still.

For this is love and nothing else is love,
The which it is reserved for God above
To sanctify to what far ends He will,
But which it only needs that we fulfill.

PRAY IN MAY

Today the birds are singing and
The grass and leaves are green,
And all the gentle earth presents
A bright and sunny scene.
It is the merry month of May
When flowers bloom once more,
And there are hopes and happy dreams
And promises in store.
What time could be more wisely spent
Than this the first of May
To say that we are thankful for
Our blessings every day?
To give our gratitude to God
In humbleness and prayer

And offer deeds of charity
As incense in the air?
Then let us love our neighbor and
Our rich and fruitful sod,
And let us go to church today
And thank almighty God.

However similar these two poems in idea, there is no comparison between them as poetry. *A Prayer in Spring* is poetry of a high order; *Pray in May* is not poetry at all. Only two qualities distinguish it from the most commonplace prose: it is written in meter, and it rhymes.

Let us examine the two poems first for their imagery. A good poem, ordinarily, is concrete: it makes an appeal to the senses. And *by* appealing to the senses, it evokes emotion from the reader.

Almost the only semblance of imagery in *Pray in May* is contained in the first six lines; the remaining fourteen, with one exception, are completely bare—better say barren. They are plain prose statements arranged metrically with a dash of rhyme. But how much imagery is there even in the first six lines? There are birds, we are told, and the birds are singing. What *kind* of birds are they? and *how* do they sing? Do they chirp, trill, whistle, peep, flute? We know only that they are birds and that they sing. Then there is grass, and there are leaves, and the grass and the leaves are green. Here indeed—if we may indulge in permissible irony—is a fresh and striking observation! Notice the arresting quality of the thought! the exact choice of words! the fresh unclouded vision of the poet! What else are we told? The day is bright and sunny, and the flowers are blooming. What *kind* of flowers? And where *is* the poet? Is he in the country or the city? in the yard? in a park? in a forest? in a meadow? We cannot tell. There is not one specific image, not one sharp detail, not one striking word to focus the reader's imagination or etch a memorable picture on the tablet of his mind. There are only generalities. "Today the birds are singing and the grass and leaves are green. . . ." *"Roses are red, violets are blue. . . ." Today the wind is blowing, and the sun is in the sky; the birds are singing in the trees, and grass is growing high. . . .* "Why," said Touchstone in Shakespeare's *As You Like It,* "I'll rhyme you so eight years together." There is nothing here, except meter and spelling, beyond the reach of the average high school freshman. We look for some freshness of vision, some originality of expression, and what do we find? "It is the merry month of May." A quaintly alliterative phrase,—but so trite and time-worn as no longer to retain a spark of fire. These are the words of a tired poet, too jaded to see life through his own eyes, comfortably content to re-use the lifeless stereotypes of versifiers for generations before him.

Now let us look at *A Prayer in Spring*. This time we need not ask where the poet is. He is in his orchard. He is a farmer, or a poet on a farm. He grows fruit for the market; he possibly collects honey from the bees; and he has to think about the harvest, but not today. What kind of trees are in his orchard? They are apple-trees, for they are in blossom, and they are white. Uniquely beautiful— "like nothing else by day"—at night they are like ghosts. Here is the first sharply-etched picture for the reader—the apple-trees, masses of blossom, gleaming white and ghostly in the moonlight. One sees oneself at night in the orchard, gazing in silence at the weird, almost eerie beauty, and feeling the whole scene to be somehow unreal.

The next two lines present another image, that of bees swarming in the trees. Here the force of the image is carried almost wholly in one happily-chosen word— the word "dilating." What does "dilating" mean? It means *swelling, expanding in size*—with the connotation of growing beyond normal. And what does a swarm of bees do? It seems to swell, then shrink, then swell some more. And all the time the bees are buzzing around it and coming from all directions and adding themselves to it. It is like the way one's head feels when he has a severe headache. The head seems to grow larger and larger, then shrink, then swell again. And all the time there is a throbbing and humming, like the bees around the swarm. The word "dilating" is fresh, precise, and potent with suggestion.

But the third stanza contains the most vivid image of all. Notice, this is not just a bird singing—any kind of bird. It is a very specific bird—a humming-bird— and its actions are described so minutely and exactly, though in only four lines, that its identity is unmistakable even though it is never named. The word "darting," the word "thrusts"—both of them perfectly chosen words for the sudden starts and pauses of a humming-bird's flight; the high-pitched humming sound heard above the bees; the needle bill; the comparison to a meteor; and the action of seeming to stand still in mid air off a blossom (its wings vibrating so fast as to be almost invisible)—all serve to picture a humming-bird so accurately and sharply that there is no need of a caption to tell us what the picture is. It is a perfect miniature. There are few such vivid pictures of the humming-bird in all English literature.

We need pause here only a moment to notice that the images so far presented are not a miscellaneous and heterogeneous collection tossed haphazardly together. They possess a simple and logical unity. The orchard is in blossom, and the blossoms attract both the bees and the humming-bird. The images belong together, and are the salient features in the scene of beauty and happiness that confronts the speaker.

Figurative language plays an important role in creating this imagery. The comparison of the blossoming trees at night to ghosts is, of course, a simile; and its use not only sharpens the image for the reader's eye but also exercises his imagination and gives him pleasure in recognizing the like elements in things otherwise quite unlike. The comparison of the humming-bird to a meteor is a metaphor—a happy one, for the bird and the meteor both go through the air with such a rush of speed that they leave an almost visible trail, a streak, behind them. The word "needle," describing the humming-bird's bill, is another metaphor. Two other figures in the poem are less obvious. When the poet says, "Keep us here all simply in the springing of the year," he means, of course, keep our *thoughts* here: Let us not profane this perfect day by worrying about the uncertainties of the harvest far off in the future. The word "us" is a metonymy, or synecdoche, in which the whole is used for the part. And what about "the orchard white"? What quality is there about this phrase that pleases our imaginations while we simply shrug our shoulders when the other poet asserts that the grass is green? Simply that this phrase is figurative, the other, literal. It is not strictly speaking the orchard that is white: the apple-blossoms are white. But the whiteness of the blossoms lends an impression of whiteness to the whole orchard, and the metonymy (again, a use of the whole for the part) conveys an imaginative truth.

The poem *Pray in May* contains one figure of speech. The line "Offer deeds of charity as incense in the air" contains a simile; and this one line is as close—though it is not very close—as this poet ever comes to poetry.

So much for the imagery of the two poems; let us turn to their music. *Pray in May* is written in iambic tetrameter lines alternating with iambic trimeter, with alternate lines rhyming. *A Prayer in Spring* is written in iambic pentameter with every line rhyming. There is a greater use of alliteration and similar devices ("merry month of May," "hopes-happy," "sunny scene," etc.) in *Pray in May*, and a greater use of rhyme in *A Prayer in Spring*. So far we have said little. It may not be superfluous, however, to point out an onomatopoetic effect in the second stanza of *A Prayer in Spring*. There is no great credit, perhaps, in using a buzzing sound when talking about *bees*. One cannot say *bees* without buzzing! But the poet has taken advantage of this fortuitous circumstance by making the word a rhyme word. When he follows *bees* with *trees* in the next line, the effective value of the sound is doubled, and we begin to hear as well as see the swarm.

It is when we analyze the poems metrically, however, or indeed when we even read them aloud, that the tremendous distance between them becomes inescapably obvious. *Pray in May* is written in unvarying iambics from start to finish. With the dubious exception of one foot, there is not a single deviation from the basic pattern. The temptation is almost overpowering to read the poem in a soporific sing-song:

To-DAY the BIRDS are SING-ing AND
The GRASS and LEAVES are GREEN,
And ALL the GENT-le EARTH pre-SENTS
A BRIGHT and SUN-ny SCENE. . . .

Such a reading is unfair. Yet the fact remains that the words seem to fall mechanically into a jog-trot pace. The one deviation from the rigid pattern is a possible trochaic substitution in the first foot of the fifth line. An intelligent reader, wishing to do his best for the poem, would read: "IT is the merry month of May." On the evidence of the rest of the poem, however, the suspicion is almost overpowering that the author himself would read it: "It IS the merry month of May."

Where the music of *Pray in May* is mechanical and monotonous, the music of *A Prayer in Spring* is subtle and varied. Any poem, of course, may be made ridiculous by bad reading; but *A Prayer in Spring* cannot be read with the steady tick-tock effect that *Pray in May* invites. Yet the meter never breaks down: the unheard iambic pentameter base persists uninterrupted in the back of the reader's mind while the heard rhythm moves gracefully around it. The contrast and the interplay of the two rhythms give the music its charm.

Scansion of this poem hardly begins to indicate the variety of the modifications and the departures from its basic pattern. The variation in many lines is too subtle to be made apparent by conventional methods of diagraming; and, where there is metrical regularity, variety is obtained by breaking the sense of some of the lines in the middle, as in the third and sixth lines.

The most notable demonstration of the poet's command of meter is in the third stanza, that describing the humming-bird. In the third line of this stanza, first of all, an anapest is substituted in the second foot. The lines describe the action of the humming-bird, and the humming-bird is described as a meteor. The accented first syllable of *meteor* is followed by two quickly-pronounced unaccented syllables, and the sound of the word, emphasized by the metrical deviation, fits its meaning. The meteor flashes through the air with its bright head up front, leaving its quickly-disappearing trail behind. Next, in the same line, a spondee is substituted in the third foot. Both *thrusts* and *in* must be stressed. Here again the sound fits the meaning. The substituted foot, with its two strong syllables, "thrusts in"-to the basic metrical pattern in the same sudden way that the humming-bird thrusts into the flowers. Finally—and this is the most magical effect of all—the following line ends with two spondees in place of the usual iambs. And their effect is especially emphasized in the last foot by the fact that the alliterating words "stand" and "still" begin and end with consonant sounds that cannot be elided or run together: the two words must be pronounced distinctly and separately. What happens? The line, beginning in its usual iambic fashion, suddenly runs into a succession of four strong equally-accented syllables. It ceases its up and down rhythm and itself stands still. The bird stands still, the line stands still. The meter mimics the action of the bird. And we realize now that the marvelous picture of the humming-bird, already commented on, relies for its power not only on the accurate choice of words and apt figures of speech, but on the very sound and rhythm of the language itself. Such effects reveal poetic genius. To recognize the difference between this poem and the other, we need only glance back at the other poet's "ToDAY the BIRDS are SINGing AND / The GRASS and LEAVES are GREEN." Here there is no attempt to vary the rhythm to describe the singing of the birds, no effort to fit sound or rhythm to meaning. Birds, grass, leaves, flowers, hopes, and dreams are all stuffed into the same rigid metrical straitjacket.

It remains that we say something about the prose meanings of the two poems. On the surface, these meanings are clear enough, and substantially the same. Both poets make the peace and beauty of nature in the spring an occasion for expressing gratitude and appreciation in prayer. On further analysis, however, we find subtle but important differences. We also run into difficulties of interpretation.

We run into difficulties, that is, in reading *A Prayer in Spring;* for, let us admit it, *Pray in May* is much easier to understand. Its meaning is plain, its language clear; it offers no problems. If ease of understanding is a criterion of merit; then *Pray in May* must get the prize.

But unless we are prepared to rank "Roses are red, violets are blue" as a greater poem than *Hamlet,* we will do well to proceed with caution. Make no mistake! Good poetry makes demands on the reader. It seeks to exercise his mind, not to relax it. It seeks to draw forth a fresh emotional response, not a stock response. It does not attempt, as Browning once said, to be a substitute for a good cigar and an easy chair for an idle man after supper. That a poem is difficult is in itself no reason to condemn it, nor that it is easy a reason to praise it. Only if, after energetic application, we find in it no depth of meaning or subtlety of emotion, or find that the meaning and emotion might have been as fully communicated in easier language, are we justified in criticizing a poem for its difficulty.

Pray in May says, in effect:

> Today it is Spring, and all nature is beautiful and happy. Let us show our gratitude to God by doing good deeds, by loving our neighbor, and by going to church.

A Prayer in Spring, after some thought, may be reasonably paraphrased thus:

> Let us take pleasure today in the beautiful gifts of nature— the orchard in blossom, the bees, and the humming-bird. On such a perfect day it would be ingratitude not to appreciate this beauty simply and fully: it would be almost sacrilege to worry about the frosts and blights that may come to spoil the harvest. By simply enjoying these gifts we show our gratitude. Such enjoyment and appreciation are love, for love means taking joy in some thing or person, and there is no true love without joy. This love God may sanctify to whatever distant and unknown purposes He wishes. Our duty is simply to

fulfill this love, to appreciate fully the beauty before us. We ourselves must answer our own prayer.

Having thus paraphrased the content of the two poems, let us now express a judgment. The paraphrasable meaning of *A Prayer in Spring* is profounder and more significant on at least three scores.

First of all, *A Prayer in Spring* has a unity of idea and a consistency of development that the other poem lacks. We are asked to take enjoyment in the beauty of nature. Such enjoyment, we are told, is equivalent to love, and we show our love to God simply by our enjoyment and appreciation of his gifts. The idea hangs together. It is initiated in the first stanza, is made concrete by specific examples in the second and third stanzas, and is brought to a climax and made complete by the generalization of the fourth. The poem is all of a piece.

In *Pray in May*, on the other hand, we are asked to show our gratitude for the beauty of nature, not by enjoying it, but by engaging in a number of unrelated activities. We are to pray, to do good deeds, to love our neighbors, and to go to church. All these activities may be excellent ways of showing our gratitude to God; they nevertheless detract from the unity of idea shown in the other poem. In one poem we show our gratitude for nature simply by loving nature. In the other poem we show it by loving something else.

In the second place, the author of *A Prayer in Spring* shows a much more mature judgment of life than the author of *Pray in May*. The judgment in *Pray in May* is sugary, conventional, and out of accord with the facts. "Life is beautiful," it says. "Not only is this day bright and sunny, but the whole month of May is 'merry.' There are hopes and happy dreams and promises in store. God gives us 'our blessings every day.' " God's in His Heaven, of course, and "all's right with the world."

The author of *A Prayer in Spring*, in contrast, indicates merely that here is one perfect day—one fair day, as another poet has said, "in a land where all days are not fair." This poet knows that life contains tragedy as well as happiness, and he does not falsify life by cutting it to the pattern of a pink-and-white lace valentine or a ten-cent-store Christmas card. He does not falsify his poetry, in other words, by prettifying life. The contrast of the two poems is brought to the touchstone by placing side by side one phrase from each—the "promises in store" of *Pray in May* and the "uncertain harvest" of *A Prayer in Spring*. For the one poet the future has nothing but promise and every story has a happy ending. The other poet knows that the future is uncertain and unknown: the crop may be a bumper crop; or it may be a failure, bringing hunger and hardship.

Finally, *Pray in May* concludes with one of the most bathetic anti-climaxes in literature. After being urged to do deeds of charity and to love our neighbors—both of them lofty and universally meritorious activities—we are told to—guess what?—"go to church." One can hardly resist the urge to put after the line, in brackets, the words "Free Advertisement." In several ways the injunction is inappropriate. First, there is its incongruity. We are told to show our gratitude for the beauty of nature by going indoors. Second, though meant for a tribute, it seems almost a reflection on the glory of God. In *A Prayer in Spring* we show our gratitude by a full appreciation of God's gifts. In this poem we must shut ourselves up and *tell* God we are grateful. And third, as a conclusion after the injunctions to good deeds and neighborly love, it comes like a squirt from a water-pistol after two shots from a cannon.

In summary, *A Prayer in Spring* is the superior poem on many counts. In imagery it is sharp and specific, where the other is abstract and general. In rhythm it is subtle and various, where the other is mechanical and monotonous. It so fits sound to meaning that the reader hears the bees and sees the flight of the humming-bird; the other makes the singing of the birds sound more like a clock. Finally, its thought-content has a unity, a maturity, and a universality that are absent from the other poem, which is sentimental.

Perhaps all these differences may be summed up in one symbolic statement. One poem *tells* us to go and pray. The other poem *is* a prayer.

Note: *A Prayer in Spring* is by Robert Frost. *Pray in May* is by James J. Metcalfe, whose daily poems were syndicated in newspapers across the United States in the 1940s and 1950s.

The Fainting Robin
vs. the Overcoat of Clay

IF I CAN STOP ONE HEART FROM BREAKING

If I can stop one heart from breaking,
I shall not live in vain;
If I can ease one life the aching,
Or cool one pain,
Or help one fainting robin
Unto his nest again,
I shall not live in vain.

Emily Dickinson

DEATH IS A DIALOGUE

Death is a dialogue between
The spirit and the dust.
"Dissolve," says Death. The Spirit, "Sir,
I have another trust."

Death doubts it, argues from the ground.
The Spirit turns away,
Just laying off, for evidence,
An overcoat of clay.

Emily Dickinson

Emily Dickinson was a great poet. But great poets are not great poets all the time. Some of them—Wordsworth is a notable example—are even bad poets much of the time. We cannot judge the merit of a poem simply by knowing who wrote it.

Of the two poems which confront us by Emily Dickinson, one is commonplace; it could have been written, if not by Tom, Dick, or Harry, at least by Ella, Grace, or Adelaide. It has nothing particular to recommend it except, perhaps, its idea—and even there we must make some qualification. The other, whether or not we call it a great poem, shows an imaginative power, a dramatic force, and an economy of expression that come only with great poetic gifts. It could not have been written by an ordinary talent.

If I Can Stop One Heart from Breaking is the commonplace poem. It is not particularly bad. But it is not particularly good. It is mediocre. Yet it *is* popular.

It has appeared in many anthologies which include work by Emily Dickinson and has, in fact, been reprinted much more often than *Death Is a Dialogue*. Why?

The explanation is that it expresses, with the adornment of rhyme and meter and a touch of sentimentality, an idea which is attractive to a great many people. Readers who go to poetry for pretty ideas rather than for poetry—the kind who like little embroidered slogans and framed proverbs on their walls: signs saying "Think" and samplers proclaiming "There's No Place Like Home"—in short, "message-hunters"—are attracted to this poem. They are attracted to it, not by the quality of the poetry but by its message. For the poem does express a noble ethical concept: that doing good to others makes life meaningful. This concept is expressed, however, with little originality or imaginative power. The poem simply *states* its idea, and in the first three lines states it rather tritely in referring to "breaking" hearts and "aching" lives. Two touches redeem the poem from complete prosaicness and give it some poetic quality. In the phrase "cool one pain" the word "cool" is both more original and more suggestive than the more usual words "soothe" or "alleviate," for it means what they do and more besides. It calls up suggestions of the fevered brow and of the burning, piercing quality of some pain, all of which will be cooled as the pain is alleviated. The freshness of the word shocks us into visualizing pain, as "soothe" and "alleviate" do not. The second poetic touch is the concrete detail of helping the fainting robin into his nest again, which saves the poem from complete generality. But although this detail does introduce a badly-needed image into the poem, it also introduces sentimentality. For the basic philosophical concept of the poem is quite worthy and intellectually respectable: one can argue and argue seriously that service rendered to others makes life worthwhile, and even that no life is really worthwhile unless it does include some good done to others; but to illustrate this philosophy with the example of helping a fainting robin into its nest is to exaggerate, to make the whole philosophy rather silly. To help a fainting robin into its nest is undoubtedly a worthy project, but to make it justify a life is to sentimentalize over robins. Possibly this statement should be taken as symbolical, but, if so, the poet has chosen an unfortunate symbol. Fainting robins and breaking hearts belong to the lace-valentine school of poetry; they should be tied up in a blue ribbon and put up in an attic trunk.

Death Is a Dialogue is also philosophical. It declares the poet's belief (at least her belief at the time of writing the poem) that the human soul is immortal. But instead of presenting us with a dry abstract statement, as the first poem almost does, this poem dramatizes its content, presents us with a little playlet, a debate, in which the body denies the reality of immortality, and the soul asserts it. The issue of immortality—which has been debated for thousands of years—is presented in a new and fresh manner, and takes on new life. It is made concrete and given imaginative appeal through the use of metaphor and personification. Death and Spirit, personified, become the antagonist and protagonist respectively of this little drama. Death is also metaphorically presented as a dialogue. And the poem ends with a brilliant metaphor when the protagonist lays off the body as "an overcoat of clay." Even what seems at first a logical confusion in the poem turns out, upon closer examination, to have poetic justification. Death, we are told in the first two lines, is a dialogue between the spirit and the dust—i.e., clay, or the body, which turns to dust. But in the next line Death appears as one of the speakers. Can Death be both the dialogue and one of the participants *in* the dialogue? But the shift of speaker from *dust* to *Death* is appropriate, for the poet is indicating the identity, really, of the two. It is only the body which dies, which returns to dust, which knows death—and thus dust and death are aspects of each other. Death, then, commands the spirit to dissolve, for it knows of no life beyond the dissolution of the body. But the Spirit refuses—"I have another trust"—namely, eternity. Death, or the body, doubts this, for it is composed of matter, and thinks that spirit depends upon matter. It argues from the ground, its natural resting place. But the Spirit triumphantly demonstrates its independence of the body by laying it off, as a man lays off an overcoat.

Insofar as their *ideas* are concerned, there is little to choose between these two poems. Neither the idea that life is justified and made meaningful by good deeds, nor the belief that there is life for the soul after death, is original or profound. But insofar as the *expression* of these ideas is concerned, there is a world of difference. The first poem makes its statement as a statement, somewhat trite, and in its illustration is somewhat sentimental. The second expresses its idea with originality, imaginative appeal, and dramatic force. For the poetry-lover as opposed to the message-hunter, it is a source of delight.

Two Poems on Love of Country

THE LONG VOYAGE

Not that the pines were darker there,
nor mid-May dogwood brighter there,
nor swifts more swift in summer air;
    it was my own country,

having its thunderclap of spring,
its long midsummer ripening,
its corn hoar-stiff at harvesting,
    almost like any country,

yet being mine; its face, its speech,
its hills bent low within my reach,
its river birch and upland beech
    were mine, of my own country.

Now the dark waters at the bow
fold back, like earth against the plow;
foam brightens like the dogwood now
    at home, in my own country.

BREATHES THERE THE MAN

Breathes there the man, with soul so dead,
Who never to himself hath said,
    This is my own, my native land!
Whose heart hath ne'er within him burned,
As home his footsteps he hath turned,
    From wandering on a foreign strand?
If such there breathe, go, mark him well;
For him no minstrel raptures swell;
High though his titles, proud his name,
Boundless his wealth as wish can claim—
Despite those titles, power, and pelf,
The wretch, concentered all in self,
Living, shall forfeit fair renown,
And, doubly dying, shall go down

To the vile dust from whence he sprung,
Unwept, unhonored, and unsung.

The Long Voyage is neither famous itself nor by a famous poet. It will probably not prove immortal. It is nevertheless a genuinely moving poem and a beautiful one, and it expresses a universal emotion. *Breathes There the Man* is a famous piece of rhetoric by a famous writer which has been memorized by thousands of schoolchildren in this and other lands. It has little to offer the mature reader. It is marked by "sound and fury" rather than by genuine substance. Let us examine the two poems one at a time.

The Long Voyage arises from a specific situation and expresses a personal feeling. The poet, or speaker, is on a ship which is rapidly taking him away from his native country. As is natural in such a situation, a powerful feeling of nostalgia—even of homesickness—arises in him for the land he loves and is leaving. The emotion is made convincing in a number of ways. First, it is expressed almost entirely through images. The poet does not speak in abstract terms of his country. Instead he calls up concrete pictures of its hills, its trees, its birds, and its changing appearance in the cycling seasons from "its thunderclap of spring" to "its corn hoar-stiff at harvesting." The emotion is also convincing because it is uttered in a quiet voice. The poet doesn't exclaim about the emptiness in his heart, the tears in his eyes, or the anguish in his soul. Nor does he make exaggerated claims for his country. He doesn't call it grander, finer, more beautiful than other countries. He grants that its pines are no darker, its dogwood no brighter, its swifts no swifter than those in other countries, and that the cycle of the seasons there is like "almost any country." But this is *his* country, and that makes the difference. He feels the affection for it that nearly all people feel for home. It is almost like a person to him: he knows and loves "its face, its speech"; and now that he is leaving it, he cannot dismiss it from his mind. The very water folding back against the prow of the ship reminds him of its earth breaking against the plow, and the very foam on the water reminds him of its bright dogwood in mid-May.

Breathes There the Man, in contrast, arises from no specific situation; it deals entirely in generalities. It is talking about no particular man and no particular situation. The poet is not expressing his own feeling for his country but his scorn for a hypothetical man who has no feeling for his country. There are no images in the poem—no sights or sounds or smells. The language is abstract. Yet the poem is not spoken quietly, but rather at the top of the poet's voice. It is even shrill. The tone is oratorical, as established by the diction and the very construction of the sentences ("Breathes there the man...," "Go, mark him well," "High though his titles...," etc.) The language is swelling ("Go, mark him well" for "See him," "Shall go down to the vile dust from which he sprung" for "Shall die"). In fact, the whole poem reminds one of a Fourth of July oration: one can imagine the orator's arms flailing the air. He is "carried away"—as a poet should be—but he is carried away by the sound of his own words rather than by deep emotion. He speaks of "foreign strands," of "minstrel raptures," of "power, and pelf," and of "fair renown." The word "shore" is more familiar than "strand," and the word "money" is more familiar than "pelf," but neither of these common words sounds impressive enough to him. Climbing by these rungs up the ladder of his own eloquence, he rises to new heights of stinging scorn and denunciation. He calls his unfeeling victim a "wretch, concentered all in self" who "doubly dying" shall go down to "vile dust" and be buried "unwept, unhonored, and unsung." There is no denying that the last line rings out with a brave sound.

But what is the occasion for all this froth and rant, this virtuous indignation and scorn? Why does our poet lash himself into such a frenzy? What is it to him that another person does not share with him an after-all-irrational feeling toward his native land? Is it any concern of his? For the feeling of patriotism *is* irrational; and this the first poet admits: his country is no more beautiful than other countries, he can explain his feeling for it only on the basis that it is his own. The second poet, however, seems almost to feel that there ought to be a law compelling people to love their country. But can love be compelled? And if a person has the misfortune to be born in a place that he does not love, is his "offense" worthy of our stinging contempt and our consignment of him to the "vile dust"?—or ought we not rather to show him our compassion? Must we hunt him down, stand around to watch him writhe in the coils of his agony, and then spit on his grave? Is not this the kind of super-heated nationalism that leads to witch-burnings and wars?

And is there any truth in the poet's picture of the man's degradation? Does the man who lacks feeling for his country of origin inevitably "forfeit fair renown," die "doubly," and go to his grave "unwept"? Is such a man necessarily a "wretch, concentered all in self"? Surely men exist who have voluntarily left their countries of birth and found places to live which they liked better—whose hearts have not "burned" when they returned to the original country—and who have nevertheless lived decent lives, loved their families, been kind to babies, and been mourned by friends when they died. The poet of *Breathes There the Man* has distorted the facts of life.

In summary, *The Long Voyage* speaks quietly but voices genuine emotion. The emotion arises honestly from a specific occasion, is expressed through images, and does not exaggerate. *Breathes There the Man* rings resoundingly but also rings hollow, like an empty drum. Its emotion does not well up naturally and spill over. It is rather an unnatural over-virtuous frenzy which the poet has whipped up, and whipped himself up to, by means of words.

Note: *The Long Voyage* is by Malcolm Cowley. *Breathes There the Man* is taken from the opening of Canto VI of *The Lay of the Last Minstrel* by Sir Walter Scott. While the excerpt expresses sentiments dramatically appropriate to the minstrel who sings the *Lay*, they are not distinguished from sentiments that could be Scott's own. The lines are frequently reprinted separately as a patriotic poem.

Are Tears Made of Sugar or of Salt?

LITTLE BOY BLUE

The little toy dog is covered with dust,
  But sturdy and staunch he stands;
And the little toy soldier is red with rust,
  And his musket moulds in his hands.
Time was when the little toy dog was new,
  And the soldier was passing fair;
And that was the time when our Little Boy Blue
  Kissed them and put them there.

"Now, don't you go till I come," he said,
  "And don't you make any noise!"
So, toddling off to his trundle-bed,
  He dreamt of the pretty toys;
And, as he was dreaming, an angel song
  Awakened our Little Boy Blue—
Oh! the years are many, the years are long,
  But the little toy friends are true!

Ay, faithful to Little Boy Blue they stand,
  Each in the same old place—
Awaiting the touch of a little hand,
  The smile of a little face;
And they wonder, as waiting the long years through
  In the dust of that little chair,
What has become of our Little Boy Blue,
  Since he kissed them and put them there.

THE TOYS

My little Son, who looked from thoughtful eyes
And moved and spoke in quiet grown-up wise,
Having my law the seventh time disobeyed,
I struck him, and dismissed
With hard words and unkissed,
His Mother, who was patient, being dead.

Then, fearing lest his grief should hinder sleep,
I visited his bed,
But found him slumbering deep,
With darkened eyelids, and their lashes yet
From his late sobbing wet.
And I, with moan,
Kissing away his tears, left others of my own;
For, on a table drawn beside his head,
He had put, within his reach,
A box of counters and a red-veined stone,
A piece of glass abraded by the beach,
And six or seven shells,
A bottle with bluebells,
And two French copper coins, ranged there with careful art,
To comfort his sad heart.
So when that night I prayed
To God, I wept, and said:
Ah, when at last we lie with trancèd breath,
Not vexing Thee in death,
And thou rememberest of what toys
We made our joys,
How weakly understood
Thy great commanded good,
Then, fatherly not less
Than I whom Thou hast moulded from the clay,
Thou'lt leave Thy wrath, and say,
"I will be sorry for their childishness."

Little Boy Blue is a poem beloved of our childhood. It served us well in the awakening years of our interest in poetry, and we cherish it accordingly. Its melody is pleasant, and so are its rhymes. The word order is natural and unforced, and so are the words themselves. The poem makes effective use of alliteration and other poetic devices. The picture it presents of the loyal toy soldier and dog awaiting the return of their Little Boy Blue is appealing and touching. The poem is skillfully done. We loved it as children, and we honor it still because we loved it then. But now we have grown up, and have put away childish things. We have tied up *Little Boy Blue* with a little blue ribbon and have put it up in the garret with our first puppy love letters, similarly tied. We have moved on to the world of adult experience, as represented by *The Toys*.

The difference between the two poems is the difference between sentimentality and honesty in emotion. The sentimental poet has his eye primarily on his reader: he wishes to draw tears from his reader and he manipulates his material to this end; that is to say, he over-simplifies it, he pretties it up and sweetens it, he subtly falsifies it by dimming the darker colors and brightening up the warmer ones. The honest poet, on the other hand, has his eye primarily on life: he wishes faithfully to record his experience of life, and he uses his material honestly to this end. The honest poet, too, may draw tears; but he does so because he has conveyed a felt emotion honestly, and not because he has contrived his material toward this effect.

Little Boy Blue is a sentimental poem. If not quite saccharine, it is certainly overly sweet. First of all, it has a sweet title. The little boy who died is not Bobby, or Peter, or Donald; he is "Little Boy Blue"—the name has nursery rhyme associations. And he has not only a sweet name, but also a sweet disposition. He played nicely with his little toys on the evening of the night he died (though he must have been sick, and most children are short-tempered and hard to manage when sick), and then he toddled sweetly off to bed at the appointed time, without a single protest, quite contrary to ordinary boy-nature. If Boy Blue ever had fits of ill temper or disobedience or crying, they are not mentioned; only his pretty actions are mentioned. But, oh dear, we have just committed an unforgivable error! We have mentioned Boy Blue without prefacing his name with the adjective "Little." For not only is Boy Blue "little," his hands are "little," his face is "little," his chair is "little," his toys are "little." The "little toy friends" await "the touch of a little hand" and "the smile of a little face." The patter of little feet did not quite get into the poem, but we surmise that they are not far outside it. At any rate the poet manages to use the adjective "little" eleven times in twenty-four lines. It is a quite superfluous word, of course, when used of a toy soldier, and is obviously being used here only to evoke the reader's sympathy. But Little Boy Blue did not die, we notice; instead he was "awakened by an angel song." It is a sweet way of describing death; the uglier features are avoided, and death becomes a rather gentle and sweetly-sad experience, like a song. Angels, of course, are another favorite property of sentimental writers—never the stern male angels of the Bible who guarded Paradise with a flaming sword, but the tender female angels of sentimentalized religious art. But anyway, Little Boy Blue was awakened, and all this happened many years ago, but the little toys are still true.

But now, three questions:

First, Little Boy Blue went to sleep and "dreamt of the pretty toys." How could we know what he dreamt about if he died in his sleep? We couldn't. Instead of reporting experience, the author is plucking at our emotions.

Second, in what sense are the toys "true"? Do they really wonder what has happened to Little Boy Blue "since he kissed them and put them there"? Or is this an example of what someone has called "the pathetic fallacy"—the fallacy of attributing human emotions to inanimate objects? That is, has not the author sentimentalized not only the little boy but also even his toys?

Third, what, after all these years, are the toys still doing where Little Boy Blue left them? Here is a question which the poet did not intend us to ask. If the toys are still in the chair where Little Boy Blue left them, his parents must have closed up his room when he died and resolved to leave everything just as he left it. People do occasionally do such things, to be sure, but only very rarely; and we usually feel that such a reaction to death is excessively sentimental or even morbid, not healthy. Quite understandably the poet glosses over this aspect of the situation and concentrates our attention instead on the supposed fidelity of the toy dog and the toy soldier, as though these qualities were what really kept them there.—In short, the author is not treating death seriously; instead he is playing with us and with our emotions.

The Toys, at first view, may seem a slightly crude poem beside Little Boy Blue. The meter is not so lilting, the rhyme is not so regular, there is no stanza pattern, and even the sentence structure seems slightly strained.* But the meter is such as to keep our attention focused constantly on the content; it does not set up a separate tune, or by a pretty lilt soften and sweeten a pathetic subject matter. Moreover, the treatment of the subject matter is honest. Having once described his son as little, the poet drops the adjective and does not use it as a spurious means of attaching sympathy to his subject. He does not idealize the behavior of little boys. Though his son is grave, quiet, and thoughtful, he is also, like most boys, sometimes repeatedly disobedient. And the father's behavior, too, as contrasted with that of the parents of Little Boy Blue, is normally human. He loses his temper, strikes the boy and scolds him, then later feels remorse and worries about what he has done. But the boy, though he has been sobbing, is not so grief-stricken that he cannot sleep, as a more sentimental writer might have made him. He is deep in slumber, his eyelashes wet; and beside his bed, to console himself, he has arranged his treasured collection of toys. These toys are enumerated and described: they include "a red-veined stone," "a piece of glass abraded by the beach," and "two French copper coins." The imagery is fresh and precise. We are not told, moreover, that the boy kissed these toys before going to sleep, or that he is dreaming of them, or that they, on their part, are faithfully waiting for him to wake up. The incident is moving because it has been honestly treated. It is a true life experience, not a sugar candy stick. Moreover, the poet has effectively used the incident to communicate, by analogy, a larger truth about life. We are all children, ultimately, and have our childish ways. We grown-up children have our grown-up toys no less foolish

---

*The syntax in lines 3-6 at first leaves some confusion as to whether dismissed takes him or His Mother as its object. Actually the confusion is effective, and may be deliberate, for both meanings are appropriate. By one construction His Mother is the subject of an absolute phrase; by the other it is the object of the verb.

really than the contents of a child's pocket. And we too disobey the Commandments of Our Father and stand equally in need of forgiveness. In referring to his son's having disobeyed "the seventh time," the poet uses a Biblical allusion to deepen and enrich his meaning further. When Peter asked Jesus how often he should forgive his brother's sinning against him, Jesus answered, Not seven times, but "seventy times seven" (Matthew 18: 21-22).

In comparing these two poems, we have been harsher with the first than we originally intended. If we had not once liked *Little Boy Blue*, we might not now be able to enjoy the maturer experience and more genuine emotion of *The Toys*. *Little Boy Blue* is a sweetly sad sentimental poem. There is certainly nothing wrong with liking it, and liking it very much, when one is young. But if one prefers this kind of poetry in maturer years, then he has ceased to grow, has become a sentimentalist himself with a sentimentalized view of life. The author of *Little Boy Blue* has spilled the sugar bowl into his poem. *The Toys*, in contrast, is preserved by the salt of genuine tears.

Note: *Little Boy Blue* is by Eugene Field. *The Toys* is by Coventry Patmore.

Capsule Comparisons

Most people talk a lot and say very little; poets talk little but say a lot. Not that good poems are necessarily shorter than other compositions; rather, they exert more pressure per linear inch. The words are selected and arranged to give each other maximal reinforcement. Each is related to its neighbors by patterns of meaning, sound, rhythm, and design. The strands in the fabric strengthen and support each other. Poems therefore *can* be very brief.

One of the briefest lyric forms, invented by those incomparable miniaturists the Japanese, is the haiku. A three-line poem, the haiku is measured by syllables rather than by stresses; its three lines are respectively five, seven, and five syllables long. Characteristically working by images rather than by statements, successful haiku (the word is both singular and plural) impress one by the quality of their observation and by their resonance. They suggest more than they say.

Undoubtedly the effectiveness of haiku is related to the genius of the Japanese temperament. The masters of the form—Bassho, Buson, Issa—are Japanese. English and American poets have also written haiku, however, and haiku —whether translated from the Japanese or composed originally in English—have found their way into English classrooms. In two ways the haiku has unique values in the classroom. Teachers have already discovered its uses in encouraging original composition. Students asked to write haiku often produce surprisingly effective results. The brevity of the form forces them to practice verbal economy, and its nature, by freeing them of the hampering notion that meter and rhyme are essential to poetry, frees them to concentrate on other dimensions of poetry. But haiku may also be effectively used in developing critical awareness. The haiku is small enough that relationships of part to whole are easily kept in mind, and critical analysis of a haiku may be thorough without becoming tiresome.

The following exercises are devised to demonstrate this possibility. In each a poem in haiku form is paired with an inferior version of itself. The problem is to identify the superior version and to explain its superiority. In each case the decision should be made on broad poetic grounds. The Japanese haiku, of course, has other aspects than those mentioned. For instance, it characteristically draws its subject from nature, and is related, at least inferentially, to a specific season of the year. It makes sparing use of such traditional poetic devices as personification, simile, and metaphor. The problem in the following exercises, however, is not to decide, according to stipulated standards, whether a certain poem is a good *haiku*, but to decide, according to poetic standards, which of two versions is a better *poem*—has greater unity, interest, and significance.

A	B
Body like a pear,	Body like a pear,
Voice like a cello—ripe, rich,	Voice like a cello—ripe, rich,
Ready to be plucked.	Waiting to be picked.

The identical opening lines of these two poems describe a lovely young woman in terms of her two outstanding features. A simile and an adjective are devoted to each comparison, the similes being linked by a submerged visual resemblance and the adjectives by alliteration. To complete the poem, a third line is needed which fulfills both of the preceding lines. Only poem A provides this. After supplying a third adjective for the alliterative series, applicable to either pear or cello, it ends with a participle having two meanings, one for pear and one for cello. Poem A thus has the compact rounded shape of its subject matter; poem B dangles.

A	B
Hypocritical	Hypocritical
Preying mantis, holy fraud,	Praying mantis, pious fraud,
You eat without grace.	You eat like a pig.

The praying mantis gets its name from its characteristic posture. With its front legs folded before it, it appears to be praying. In actuality, of course, it is crouching, ready to spring on some unsuspecting smaller insect. It uses the folded front legs to seize and hold its victim while devouring him.

Both poems focus on this discrepancy between appearance and reality. Poem B does so clumsily, however. Its climactic line is both ludicrous and trite. Poem A makes its contrast more subtly and with greater compression of meaning. The second line pivots on two puns: "preying" and *praying*, "holy" and *wholly*. Both puns serve the contrast. The third line has three meanings. The mantis eats without saying grace (*without* praying). It eats ungracefully. And it eats without being in a state of grace—that condition of soul reserved for the blessed and denied to insects and hypocrites.

A	B
A dry arroyo:	A dry arroyo:
A slender rill of water.	One thin trickle of water.
An old man speaking.	An old man talking.

The intent in both poems is the same: by putting two images side by side to suggest a likeness between them. An old man talking, these poems imply, is like a dry arroyo with a very little water running through it. Poem B, by its superior command of connotation and linkage of sound and meaning, more successfully exploits the comparison.

No two words are exact synonyms. Though "talking" and "speaking" denote the same action, "speaking" implies greater purposefulness, more formality, and an action limited in time. "Talking," which may be aimless and endless, fits better the images of the old man and of water through an arroyo. Similarly "trickle," which suggests a smaller volume of water and a less steady flow, is more appropriate than "rill" to ideas of dryness and old age. In addition, "thin" and "trickle" lack the inappropriate connotations of beauty contained in "slender" and "rill."

Meanings may be reinforced by sounds. "Thin" and "trickle" in poem B are broadly onomatopoetic: their short i sound is associated with littleness (cf. "bit," "chip," "snip," "whit," "slim," and, indeed, "rill"), and the final -le of "trickle" suggests repetition (cf. "ripple," "bubble," "rattle," "rumble," "twinkle," "sparkle"). The repeated t's and k's of "trickle" and "talking" link these two words in sound, reinforcing the implied simile between them. The rhythmical stress on the word "One" forces an appropriate emphasis on that word. In poem A the euphonious quality of the words "slender" and "rill" (with their liquid l's, r's, and n's) reinforces the inappropriate connotations of beauty in these words.

A	B
Mrs. Cardinal,	Mrs. Cardinal,
How long you sit on your nest	How long you brood on your nest
Protecting your eggs!	Over the future!

Both poems are concerned with the patience of the mother cardinal in sitting on her eggs; but the poem B makes something out of this concern, poem A does not. Except for the personification involved in whimsically apostrophizing the cardinal as "Mrs.," poem A makes a literal and unimaginative statement. The personification leads to nothing. Poem B, by using three words of dual signification, conveys meaning on two levels. On the first level, "brood" means *sit on in order to hatch*, "over" means *above*, and "future" (by the figurative process of metonymy) refers to the cardinal's eggs. On the second level, "brood" means *think gravely and deeply*, "over" means *concerning*, and "future" has its ordinary meaning. On the second level, the last two lines of the poem, by attributing human forethought to the bird, continue the personification of the first line and elevate the cardinal into a symbol for human parenthood.

A   B

The phoenix, rare bird,   The phoenix, choice bird,
Burns like a torch on the bough   Flames like a torch on the bough
Ardent for rebirth.   Eager for rebirth.

The phoenix, in ancient mythology, was a fabulous bird of which only one specimen existed in the world at a time. After a life of five hundred years it built itself a spicy nest, set the nest afire by fanning it with its wings, and burned itself alive. From its ashes sprang a new phoenix. In Christian typology the resurrected phoenix figures as a symbol of rebirth.

Poem A differs from poem B in only three words, but these three words give it a precision and a unity which poem B lacks. Though "rare" means much the same as "choice" (i.e., of unusual quality), it also underscores the scarcity of the bird which existed in a single specimen. Though "ardent" means much the same as "eager" (i.e., greatly desirous), its derivation from a Latin word meaning *burning* gives it overtones which sustain and intensify the central image of the poem. "Burns," meanwhile, is superior to "flames" because of its sound. By repeating in its first three letters the initial sounds of "bird" and "birth," it links together aurally the major concepts of the poem.

Part Three

The Poem
in Relation to
Other Human Concerns

The Poet and the Pulpit

In the year 1880, at a time when religious dogma and religious faith had for many Englishmen suffered mortal blows from the onslaught of Darwinism and scientific rationalism, Matthew Arnold, the poet and critic, made a remarkable prophecy about poetry:

> The future of poetry is immense, because in poetry where it is worthy of its high destinies, our race, as time goes on, will find an ever surer stay. There is not a creed which is not shaken, not an accredited dogma which is not shown to be questionable, not a received tradition which does not threaten to dissolve. Our religion has materialized itself in the fact, in the supposed fact, and now the fact is failing it. But for poetry the idea is everything; the rest is a world of illusion, of divine illusion. Poetry attaches its emotion to the idea; the idea *is* the fact. The strongest part of our religion to-day is its unconscious poetry.

What did Arnold mean by saying, "Religion has materialized itself in the fact, in the supposed fact, and now the fact is failing it"? He meant that the faith of most Christian believers was founded upon a literal acceptance of certain supposed historical events as facts. It was necessary not only to believe in Christ as a historical personage, but also to regard it as literally true that he was conceived by God upon a virgin, and that he rose from the dead after being buried three days. People attached emotion to these "facts," and now the "facts" were failing them. With the advance of knowledge, it was becoming harder and harder to believe any longer in the literal truth of the Virgin Birth, or of the Resurrection, or of any of the Biblical miracles. With the removal of these Christian cornerstones, the whole edifice of religious faith built upon them was swaying and toppling.

With poetry it was otherwise; for "poetry," said Arnold, "attaches its emotion to the idea"; for *it* "the idea is the fact." We do not have to believe that Achilles and Ulysses were actual personages, or that Homer's account of the Trojan War or of the travels of Ulysses are transcriptions of history, for the *Iliad* and the *Odyssey* to have value for us. It is unimportant to us whether Hamlet and King Lear ever really existed; Shakespeare's plays are not one whit less significant if they did not or one whit more significant if they did. We need not believe in the literal existence of mermaids and mermen for Arnold's own poem *The Forsaken Merman* to have meaning for us. For poetry presents a world "of divine illusion"; it is one of the realms of fiction, whose truths are independent of its "facts."

Arnold's day, of course, was a day of religious crisis; loss of faith and conversion to agnosticism was one of its most common experiences. And so, to meet this crisis, Arnold wished poetry to perform a religious function, saw it, in fact, as in the future largely replacing religion.

> More and more mankind will discover that we have to turn to poetry to interpret life for us, to console us, to sustain us. Without poetry, our science will appear incomplete; and most of what now passes with us for religion and philosophy will be replaced by poetry.

I wish I could say that Arnold's prophecy had come true. But I cannot. I see no evidence of any considerable body of men for whom poetry is serving a religious function, of any large number whom it has saved from religious chaos. Most men, in fact, do not read poetry, have never read poetry, may never read poetry. Poetry seems to be a pleasure of the few, not the many. For its full comprehension and appreciation it demands a degree of knowledge, sensitivity, intelligence, and skill that the majority of men do not possess. For most men, bread and circuses have always been a superior attraction, or, in modern terms, TV and chorus-lines.

Yet poetry *can*, for some men, perform the function that Matthew Arnold prescribed for it. It served such a function for Arnold himself. In a sonnet entitled *To a Friend*, he begins with a question: "Who prop, thou ask'st, in these bad days, my mind?" His answer to the question is Homer, Epictetus, and Sophocles—three poets (or two poets and an epigrammatist). More notably, poetry served a religious function for Arnold's elder contemporary, John Stuart Mill. Mill, during his early twenties, underwent a severe emotional and mental depression, described in his *Autobiography*, in which he "seemed to have nothing left to live for." Greatly instrumental in recovering him from this crisis was the poetry of Wordsworth.

> What made Wordsworth's poems a medicine for my state of mind, was that they expressed, not mere outward beauty, but states of feeling, and of thought coloured by feeling, under the excitement of beauty.

He singles out for special mention Wordsworth's famous ode, *Intimations of Immortality from Recollections of Early Childhood*, a poem in which he found, along with more than Wordsworth's usual "sweetness of melody and rhythm," and along with the two so-often-quoted passages "of grand imagery but bad philosophy," a description by Wordsworth of an experience similar to his own.

If, then, poetry is capable of performing a religious function, if it is able "to interpret life for us, to console us, to sustain us," in what way is it able to do this? What are the "ideas" to which poetry "attaches its emotion"? What, in short, is the nature of poetic truth?

Let us begin by examining Tennyson's famous and beautiful poem *Crossing the Bar*, in which an aged poet contemplates approaching death.

CROSSING THE BAR

Sunset and evening star,
    And one clear call for me!
And may there be no moaning of the bar,
    When I put out to sea,

But such a tide as moving seems asleep,
    Too full for sound and foam,
When that which drew from out the boundless deep
    Turns again home.

Twilight and evening bell,
    And after that the dark!
And may there be no sadness of farewell,
    When I embark;

For though from out our bourne of Time and Place
    The flood may bear me far,
I hope to see my Pilot face to face
    When I have crossed the bar.

Here, beautifully presented, is the expression of a calm, untroubled faith. The idea of approaching death, effectively conveyed through a combination of two symbols—the coming of evening and the beginning of an ocean voyage—strikes no fear in the poet. All the images, by their beauty and calm, define the poet's acceptance of death as quiet and serene: "Sunset . . . evening star . . . one clear call . . . such a tide as moving seems asleep . . . home . . . twilight . . . evening bell." The poet even requests that there may be "no moaning of the bar," that is, "no sadness of farewell" when he dies. And why not? Because, after the ship's crossing of the bar at the harbor's mouth, marking its transition from "our bourne of Time and Place" into the sea of eternity, the speaker will be "home" and will see his "Pilot face to face." There is no reason to lament his passing, for he is going on to a better world. The "hope" expressed at the end of the poem is not just hope; it is confident expectation. The poet accepts death serenely, for he is confident of immortality.

Upon closer examination, however, we discover that the poet, though confident of the *fact* of immortality, is uncertain as to its *mode*—an uncertainty which makes him hedge his bets between two different and in fact opposed conceptions. In the second stanza, when he refers to "that which drew from out the boundless deep" he is referring to his soul, which, upon death, "Turns again home"—returns, that is, to "the boundless deep"—the ocean of eternity or of universal spirit. In the fourth stanza, when he says, "I hope to meet my Pilot face to face," he is again referring to his soul, which after death will see its Creator. The first image derives from a pantheistic belief. The soul is referred to by an impersonal pronoun ("which") and is imaged as a droplet of water which at birth is separated from the ocean of boundless spirit and which at death returns to it, merging its separate identity in the divine whole. The second image suggests an anthropomorphic belief. The soul is referred to this time by a personal pronoun ("I"); it retains its separate identity after death and greets its Maker "face to face." God, here, is not an ocean of divine spirit but a person— a Pilot with a face. The two conceptions contradict each other, and reflect an uncertainty which characterized Tennyson's thought all his life. He instinctively clung to the anthropomorphic concept of the traditional Christian belief in which he had been brought up. But he found a pantheistic concept easier to reconcile with the concepts of modern science.

Clearly, if immortality is the "idea" to which this poem attaches its emotion, the idea is a vague one. But *is* certainty of immortality the "poetic truth" of this poem? *Is* immortality one of the truths of which poetry assures us? Certainly, many people have used this poem for the religious consolation and the support that Arnold said could be found in poetry. But before we accept this consolation too readily, let us look at another poem. This one is by A. E. Housman, and it is called *The Immortal Part.* In it a young man brings us an account of what his bones within him seem to say. The bones resent being the slaves of flesh and soul, forced to do their bidding and to carry them about. The bones look forward to death and their release from this bondage. Death, for them, indeed, will be a new birth. Every man, male or female—they tell the young man—is pregnant, with a skeleton. He will give birth to this skeleton at his death.

THE IMMORTAL PART

When I meet the morning beam,
Or lay me down at night to dream,
I hear my bones within me say,
'Another night, another day.

'When shall this slough of sense be cast,
This dust of thoughts be laid at last,
The man of flesh and soul be slain
And the man of bone remain?

'This tongue that talks, these lungs that shout,
These thews that hustle us about,

This brain that fills the skull with schemes,
And its humming hive of dreams,—

'These to-day are proud in power
And lord it in their little hour:
The immortal bones obey control
Of dying flesh and dying soul.

"'Tis long till eve and morn are gone;
Slow the endless night comes on,
And late to fulness grows the birth
That shall last as long as earth.

'Wanderers eastward, wanderers west,
Know you why you cannot rest?
'Tis that every mother's son
Travails with a skeleton.

'Lie down in the bed of dust;
Bear the fruit that bear you must;
Bring the eternal seed to light,
And morn is all the same as night.

'Rest you so from trouble sore,
Fear the heat o' the sun no more,
Nor the snowing winter wild,
Now you labour not with child.

'Empty vessel, garment cast,
We that wore you long shall last.
—Another night, another day.'
So my bones within me say.

Therefore they shall do my will
To-day while I am master still,
And flesh and soul, now both are strong,
Shall hale the sullen slaves along,

Before this fire of sense decay,
This smoke of thought blow clean away,
And leave with ancient night alone
The steadfast and enduring bone.

If *Crossing the Bar* was subtly in contradiction with itself, here is a poem
that contradicts both positions implicit in *Crossing the Bar*. The title is grimly
ironical, for, before we have read four stanzas, we discover that "the immortal
part" is not the soul, as we had anticipated, but the skeleton. The soul blows

away at death like a puff of smoke; "the steadfast and enduring bone" remains. The "rebirth" promised at death is not the Christian rebirth of the soul, but simply a birth of the skeleton.

Now what becomes of the consolation and sustentation that Matthew Arnold promised us in poetry as a substitute for religion? How can poetry "interpret life" for us if one poem tells us that life leads on to further life, while another poem tells us that life ends with death? Is not the "idea" of immortality simply another fact, supposed fact, or non-fact, like the Virgin Birth and the Resurrection, a supposed fact to which these two poems, in their different ways, attach emotion? One might argue, perhaps, that different kinds of people can get different kinds of comfort from different kinds of poem. In *Crossing the Bar* the believer can find support for his own hopeful faith, can learn to face death calmly by relying on his confidence in the reality of a future life. From *The Immortal Part* the unbeliever may derive a renewed stoic determination to make the most of life while he has it. Today while he is "master still," he can make his bones obey his will. But such a solution seems less than satisfactory. Unless we can define poetic truth in such a way that it makes all good poems equally available to all good readers, we probably should give up the attempt. But before we examine the problem further, let us look at one more poem. This one is by Matthew Arnold himself, and it is entitled *Dover Beach*.

Dover Beach is Arnold's lament over the decline of religious faith. The "Sea of Faith" was once at the full, he tells us—perhaps he means in the Middle Ages, or perhaps earlier in the nineteenth century before the advent of Darwinism—but now he only hears "its melancholy, long, withdrawing roar," like the sound of a wave retreating or the sound of the tide going out. The speaker in the poem is in a room overlooking the cliffs of Dover, with a pebbled beach at their foot, and the English channel beyond. Across the channel, some twenty miles or so away, he can occasionally make out the coast of France as it catches the gleam of the moonlight. In the room with him is someone dear to him, a wife or sweetheart, to whom he is unburdening his despair. The poem is built on a series of contrasts, the two principal ones being a contrast between the illusory physical beauty of the world and its actual spiritual darkness, and the contrast between the full tide which the speaker sees before him and the tide of faith, which is ebbing.

DOVER BEACH

The sea is calm tonight,
The tide is full, the moon lies fair
Upon the straits;—on the French coast the light
Gleams and is gone; the cliffs of England stand,
Glimmering and vast, out in the tranquil bay.

Come to the window, sweet is the night-air!
Only, from the long line of spray
Where the sea meets the moon-blanched land,
Listen! you hear the grating roar
Of pebbles which the waves draw back, and fling,
At their return, up the high strand,
Begin, and cease, and then again begin,
With tremulous cadence slow, and bring
The eternal note of sadness in.

Sophocles long ago
Heard it on the Aegean, and it brought
Into his mind the turbid ebb and flow
Of human misery; we
Find also in the sound a thought,
Hearing it by this distant northern sea.

The Sea of Faith
Was once, too, at the full, and round earth's shore
Lay like the folds of a bright girdle furled.
But now I only hear
Its melancholy, long, withdrawing roar,
Retreating, to the breath
Of the night-wind, down the vast edges drear
And naked shingles of the world.

Ah, love, let us be true
To one another! for the world, which seems
To lie before us like a land of dreams,
So various, so beautiful, so new,
Hath really neither joy, nor love, nor light,
Nor certitude, nor peace, nor help for pain;
And we are here as on a darkling plain
Swept with confused alarms of struggle and flight,
Where ignorant armies clash by night.

Here, I submit, is one of the most eloquent expressions of despair in
all English poetry. The speaker lives in a world drained of significance by
the decline of religious faith. Despite the illusory physical beauty of this
world, illumined by the moonlight, its actual spiritual state is one in which
there is

        . . . neither joy, nor love, nor light,
Nor certitude, nor peace, nor help for pain.

In such a world, personal love is the only thing left to cling to, and the speaker cries out in his anguish, "Ah, love, let us be true to one another!" But one is made to feel that even this love is a frail support in a vast spiritual darkness, that though the two lovers cling together, they are simply lost together rather than each alone. The final image for this spiritual world is remarkable for the way it piles up words indicating darkness, confusion, and conflict. The plain is "darkling," the "alarms" by which it is swept are "confused," they are alarms "of struggle and flight," the contending armies are "ignorant," they "clash," and they do so "by night." The picture called up is one of utter darkness, of noisy disorder and cross-purposes, where men strike against each other blindly, mistaking friend for foe in their confusion.

And now I must ask, Is this the kind of poetry in which its author felt "our race, as time goes on, will find an ever surer and surer stay"? Can we turn to this kind of poetry "to interpret life for us, to console us, to sustain us"? Is this kind of poetry capable of performing a religious function?

And here I must answer, astonishingly, "Yes!" Deliberately, "Yes!" Firmly, "Yes!" Speaking first from personal experience, let me testify that all three of these poems, so different in theme and idea, so different in the confidence with which their speakers face the present or the future—all three of these poems have enriched my own life, have in their different ways consoled or sustained me, have made my life more precious to me. (That this experience is not merely personal is evidenced by the frequency with which all three turn up in anthologies.) I will go even further. All three of these poems embody and express poetic truth. How they do so, and how they sustain me, requires some explanation. My explanation has two parts:

You will remember that what gave Wordsworth's poems medicinal value for John Stuart Mill was that they expressed "states of feeling, and of thought coloured by feeling," and that one of the best medicines in Wordsworth's kit was a poem marked by passages "of grand imagery but bad philosophy." True feelings, not true ideas, made these poems efficacious. The truth of poetry, then, lies not in the beliefs it expresses, which are matters of opinion, but in the experience it communicates, which is a matter of imagined life. Poetry cannot tell us whether or not there is immortality; it *can* tell us what men have thought and how they have felt about immortality. Thus *Crossing the Bar* truly tells us how it feels to look forward confidently at the end of a long life to a new and better life to come. *The Immortal Part* truly tells us how it feels to have discarded any such belief and to determine to live resolutely a life which will end—end utterly— with death. *Dover Beach* truly tells us how it feels to be in despair over the decline of religious faith and the presence of conflict and confusion in the world. The poetic truth of these poems applies not to the truth of the views expressed, but to the experience of having those views. Poetry, in brief, is not a means by which we improve our minds, but a means by which, imaginatively, we broaden our experience. Through poetry we live, not only our own rather narrowly constricted lives, but many widely varying lives. Through poetry we can get out of our own skins and know what it is like to be in the skins of others. Poems may be false, of course, as well as true; but poetic falsity arises when the poet is not faithful to the full complexity of his feelings, or of a dramatic character's feelings; it does not refer to the correctness of his beliefs. It thus happens that excellent poems have been written on all sides of almost every arguable question, and that all may be valued and enjoyed by a man of catholic taste. And it is thus possible for me to derive value from both *Crossing the Bar* and *The Immortal Part.*

My second point, and that which particularly explains the consolation I receive from *Dover Beach,* involves one of the fundamental paradoxes of human experience. It is this. All experience, when successfully organized and transmitted to the imagination in the form of art, is enjoyable—even painful experience. In real life death and pain and suffering are not pleasurable, but in poetry they may be. In real life unrequited love is not pleasurable, but in poetry it can be. In actual life, if we cry, usually we are unhappy; but if we cry while seeing a play or reading a poem, we are thoroughly enjoying it. The crowning paradox, indeed, is that in art, as opposed to life, the most painful experiences are often the most pleasurable. Shakespeare's tragedies communicate a deeper, more enduring joy than do his comedies, as successful as these are. "Our sweetest songs," says Shelley in *To a Skylark,* "are those that tell of saddest thought." Whether or not tragic experience, encountered in poetry, tempers and steels our souls and enables us better to endure tragic experience encountered in life, I shall not say. I think it does. But this is not the point. The point is that tragic experience in poetry is in itself a source of joy. It makes us more intensely alive. And human beings are so constructed as to find some value in all intense living. It is the opposite of being dead. Poetry sustains us by bringing us life, intense life, rich life, experienced through the imagination. Poetry comes to us bringing life in both hands.

Thus it is that even poems which sing eloquently of the sweetness of death, as some of our greatest poems do, are serving the claims of life. While I read, in Keats's *Ode to a Nightingale,*

> Now more than ever it seems rich to die,
>   To cease upon the midnight with no pain,

or when I hear Walt Whitman calling out, in *When Lilacs Last in the Dooryard Bloom'd,*

> Come lovely and soothing death,
> Undulate round the world, serenely arriving, arriving,

In the day, in the night, to all, to each,
Sooner or later delicate death,

or when A. E. Housman advises me, in *When Smoke Stood Up from Ludlow*,

Lie down, lie down, young yeoman;
The sun moves always west;
The road one treads to labour
Will lead one home to rest,
And that will be the best—

while, I say, I read such sweet inducements to death, or such lovely expressions of despair over life as are found in *Dover Beach*, so long do I find the savor of my own life sweeter, so long am I more tenaciously in love with life. The poets sing so lovingly of death as to make us want to live if only to hear them.

Thank you, Matthew Arnold. I will not claim, nor do I think would you, that poetry is the only source of religious value, or that poetry must entirely replace religion. There are certainly many other sources of religious joy and consolation, and religion has its own values when disencumbered of its dead "facts" —of beliefs no longer tenable. We claim—Matthew and I—only that poetry does serve a religious function, that it embodies a form of truth, and that it is capable, in its own way, of interpreting life for us, of consoling us, and sustaining us. For Poetry says, with Christ, and says it sweetly and invitingly, "I am come that ye may have life, and that ye may have it more abundantly."

The Poet and the Laboratory

We live, we are often told, in an age of science. We have seen during our life-times the invention of the hydrogen bomb and the first landing of men on the moon. There may be a connection between these events.

In the hydrogen bomb, scientists have invented a means of explosion capable of eliminating one of the planets from the universe as a place fit for human habitation. Having done this, it's appropriate that they should look for some place else for man to go. Space exploration seems the necessary corollary of the discovery of nuclear fission.

A frequent deduction from this situation is that we must educate more en-gineers and scientists, in order to keep up, or catch up, with Russia. The reason for this need is obvious: it's so that we can blow the Russians up before they blow us up. Nowhere, on the other hand, do we hear it said that what we need is more poets and readers of poetry. Yet if America and Russia were engaged in a race to see which could turn out more first-rate poets rather than more nu-clear scientists, the world might be a far safer place to live in.

What is the need for poetry in an age of science? In this paper I'd like to ex-plore some of the differences between science and poetry and to explain why I think both are necessary. I won't claim that we don't need more engineers and scientists. I *will* claim that, more imperatively, we need more good poets and readers of poetry. What do we need fewer of? Well, salesmen possibly—juvenile delinquents certainly.

First, what do I mean by poetry? I do not necessarily mean that peculiar kind of writing which is printed in lines of irregular length going down the page instead of that neater kind which always keeps equal margins. I mean rather a kind of writing whose primary concern is to extend and deepen the range of human experience, whose function is to make us more *alive*, and by doing so to make us more *human*.

I ask children sometimes, "What is the opposite of poetry?" The answer comes back, "Prose." But the opposition of prose and poetry is a false one. The opposite of prose is not poetry, but verse. Prose is the well-scrubbed, well-behaved kind of writing that keeps equal margins. Verse has more internal order, but has no respect for margins. *Poetry* may be written in prose or verse. *Moby-Dick* and *The Old Man and the Sea* are poetry; and so, by my definition, are *Huckleberry Finn* and *The Death of a Salesman*. When a piece of writing conveys some aspect of human experience with intensity or passion, it becomes poetry.

If the opposite of prose is verse, then *what* is the opposite of poetry? Let me suggest just a tentative answer. The opposite of poetry is science. Science and poetry take opposite approaches to experience. Science is the *analysis* of experience, poetry is the *synthesis* of experience. Science is the taking apart of experience in order to know it piece by piece. Poetry is the putting together of experience in order to know it in its totality.

How, for instance, might the poet and the scientist approach the experience of water? The poet might tell you a number of things about water. Water is clear and silvery; it sparkles in the sunlight. Water is transparent: you can see the face of your sweetheart through a glass of it. Water reflects: you can look into a pool of water and see your own face in it. Water is cool to the skin; when you dip an arm into it, it mats the hair and leaves your skin wet. Water is refreshing: you can quench your thirst with it. When water is gathered in lakes or oceans, it becomes blue or green in color. It reflects the sky and the clouds. Water bears you up: you can swim in it. Sometimes water becomes wrinkled or gathered in waves which pound on the rocks and break up in spray. Water may be cruel: a man can drown in it.

And how does the scientist approach water? For the scientist, water is a chemical compound of which the individual molecules consist of two atoms of hydrogen and one of oxygen. In scientific shorthand, water equals H_2O.

Of course, the scientist can tell us other things about water, too. He tells us its density and specific gravity, its boiling point and its freezing point, its refractive index, its coefficient of thermometric conductivity, and its dielectric constant—whatever that is. But in all cases, the scientist is interested in something less than the total experience of water, and is interested in it one aspect at a time. As far as possible he holds all the variables constant except one, so that he can study that one variable, that one abstracted aspect, in isolation. And what he finally gives us is a fact *about* water, or a series of facts about water; he does not, like the poet, reproduce the whole shining experience of water intact and alive in the imagination. When the scientist tells us that water is H_2O, he tells us something that no poet would ever have discovered. But when Tennyson writes,

> All night
> The plunging seas draw backward from the land
> Their moon-led waters white,

or when Matthew Arnold describes how

> the stars perform their shining,
> And the sea its long moon-silvered roll,

they are equally describing a truth about water—a truth beyond the reach of the scientist as scientist.

"Science," says Robert Louis Stevenson, "writes of the world as if with the cold finger of a starfish; it is all true; but what is it when compared to the reality of which it discourses? where hearts beat high in April, and death strikes, and hills totter in the earthquake, and there is a glamour over all the objects of sight, and a thrill in all noises for the ear, and Romance herself has made her dwelling among men?"

Here, then, is a first difference between science and poetry. Science is the *analysis* of experience, is interested in its aspects one by one. Poetry is the *synthesis* of experience, is interested in it as those aspects fit together to form a totality.

But there is another important difference. The poet, when he tells us about water, tells us how it appears *to* the human being. You can see your face reflected in it or your sweetheart's face refracted through it. It is cool to your skin, it mats your hair, it quenches your thirst, it bears you up, it can drown you. What color is water? Is water blue? Not for the scientist. For the scientist water reflects light waves of certain frequencies and absorbs light waves of other frequencies. Its *blue-ness*, the experience of blue-ness, originates in the observer's head. And so science tries to separate the thing observed from the observer; it is interested only in the thing-ness of the thing, while poetry is interested in it as it affects our humanity.

The human being, indeed, is an embarrassment to the scientist. It would be best if he could be eliminated. The scientist must be objective. He must measure and weigh and count. And so the scientist always introduces an instrument between himself and the thing studied; he has to separate himself from it, to get as distant from it as he can. At the least he uses a ruler or a scales or a thermometer. More elaborately he may use a telescope, a microscope, a complicated electrical apparatus, a photoelectric eye, a test-tube jungle. Increasingly the scientist has to devise instruments to *use* his instruments, and other instruments to *read* his instruments. He finds, in his most delicate experiments with heat, for example, that he can no longer go up and read a thermometer, for the very approach of the human body to the thermometer violates the accuracy of the reading. Somehow he has to eliminate the human body, or keep it at a distance.

Do our astronomers walk out into the "mystical, moist night air" and look up at the stars with unaided eye? No; they use a telescope. But do they take the telescope in their *hands* and *aim* it at the stars? No; they attach the telescope to a clock and let the clock aim the telescope. Do they then look *through* the telescope and see the starlight as it falls through the lenses directly on the eye? No; the lens of the telescope is at right angles to its barrel, and the light reaches the lens only after it has been reflected by several mirrors. But do the astronomers even look *into* the telescope? No; today they put a camera at the eye-piece of the telescope and let *it* look at the stars. And how does the scientist deal with radioactive materials? He puts the materials in one room, puts himself in another room with thick glass windows between, works the controls of a mechanical crane that lifts and moves the materials, then puts his arms into a pair of heavily insulated sleeves extending into the other room, grasps some sort of tool through the heavy gloves, and with this tool does something to the materials, stirs them perhaps. In this case the scientist has to separate himself from his materials lest the human factor be eliminated in a way displeasing even to him.

For ultimately, of course, the scientist cannot entirely eliminate the human observer, as much as he might like to. There must be somebody to examine the photographs, somebody to press the buttons, somebody to read and interpret the data transcribed on the smoked revolving drum. But if the scientist cannot eliminate the human being—cannot eliminate himself—he *must* eliminate a good *part* of the human being. For if science presents but one aspect at a time of the thing it studies, it also presents it to the consideration of but one aspect of human consciousness—the intellect. All other human faculties are disturbing elements; the human factor must be minimized. Emotions are irrelevant: they upset the validity of experiments and vitiate the interpretation of results. Errors of the senses must be corrected by the use of instruments. Imagination, though useful for suggesting a procedure or a hypothesis, must be rigidly checked and counterchecked. Fancy is a wild thing and must be restrained: it might sub-stitute a unicorn for the corpse on the dissecting table; it might picture, as Hamlet does, a camel in a cloud; or, reversing things, it might see the evening stretched out against the sky as a patient etherized upon a table.

And how wrongheaded the poet is, after all! He looks up at the sky and he mutters, "The moon [is] a ghostly galleon tossed upon cloudy seas." Galleon indeed! Or he may look down into a pool and see hanging there another sky. How twisted up can one get? In a moment of greater clarity, he may look up and say with Coleridge's ancient mariner:

The moving moon went up the sky,
And nowhere did abide;
Softly she was going up,
And a star or two beside.

But even this is nonsense! When the moon seems to be moving among the clouds, the clouds are really moving in front of the moon. When the moon seems to climb up the sky, the earth is really *turning past* an unmoving moon, though the moon too has a motion which must be taken into scientific account. Surely Shakespeare did have one moment of scientific insight: when he classified the lunatic, the lover, and the poet as being all of one kind!

And yet, though so precise and accurate the scientific account, how false it is to all human experience! For science, the further it advances, the further it takes us away from the truth of human experience. The very chair on which I sit dissolves under the examination of science into a swarm of atoms, each a miniature solar system with electrons revolving like miniature planets around its central body, and each system separated from its neighbor by vast distances of space. The scientist presents us this conception as fact. I acknowledge the fact, but wonder how it manages to hold me up. For truth I return to the poet and

> The moving moon went up the sky,
> And nowhere did abide;
> Softly she was going up,
> And a star or two beside.

But I would leave a wrong impression if I let it be thought that I think ill of scientists, or that I think of science and poetry as antagonistic. Some of my best friends are scientists.

It is true that some individuals, among both scientists and poets, have thought of the two activities as antagonistic. Sir Isaac Newton is reported to have dismissed poetry as "ingenious fiddle-faddle." And William Wordsworth described a scientist as "one that would peep and botanize / Upon his mother's grave." John Keats accused Newton of reducing the rainbow to commonplaceness by reporting it as a prismatic phenomenon, and Edgar Allan Poe pictured science as a vulture, preying on the poet's heart. But wiser heads among both parties have prevailed. Tennyson, speaking of scientific knowledge in *In Memoriam* as "a beam in darkness," said, "Let it grow! / Let knowledge grow from more to more." And Charles Darwin said that if he had his life to live again, he would make it a rule to read some poetry and listen to some music at least once a week, because "the loss of these tastes is a loss of happiness, and may possibly be injurious to the intellect and more probably to the moral character, by enfeebling the emotional part of our nature."

Science and poetry are complementary, not antagonistic, activities. They should be partners, not enemies. And life is always in danger when this partnership is threatened, as it is, indeed, today. Science is, or should be, an aid *to* life. Poetry is, and ought to be, a means *of* life. Science—though it may lead to destruction—is necessary for survival. Poetry makes us worthy of survival, and makes survival worthwhile. Without science we should probably not be able to exist, or not for long. Without poetry, and music, and art, many of us should not much *want* to exist. For art makes worthwhile the extensions of life that science gives us. The use of poetry is to make us human.

To the medieval mind, interestingly enough, the poet and the scientist both figured as necromancers. Virgil, for many centuries, was set down as a mighty magician. He was supposed to have fabricated a brazen fly and an ever-blooming orchard, to have beguiled the devil, and to have built for the emperor a marvelous castle in which the emperor could see and hear everything done or said in Rome. Aristotle, and Roger Bacon, the thirteenth century scientist, were similarly regarded as magicians. Roger Bacon was supposed to have constructed a brazen head capable of talking and delivering lectures on philosophy. He also controlled devils, and meant to use them to build a wall of brass about England so that no enemy might "touch a grass of English ground." And there is little to wonder at in either superstition. For poets and scientists and magicians are all people who exercise extraordinary powers by means of spells or verbal formulas. "Abracadabra, hocus pocus," says the necromancer, and a beautiful woman is suddenly made invisible. "Arma virumque canto," begins Virgil, and the living past is conjured up before us. "$E = MC^2$," says Einstein, and Hiroshima disappears in a mushroom cloud. The people of the middle ages were not so mistaken after all. For Virgil, in a very real sense, may be said to have made "an ever-blooming garden." And scientists today have constructed brazen heads that not only speak but think. Instead of commanding devils to do their bidding, they command machines; and the machines do not only their housework—but their homework.

But machines, though they may perform complicated problems in mathematics, cannot write *King Lear*. And they cannot read it. Poetry is not outmoded by the inventions and discoveries of the age of science. Poetry is rendered even more necessary by the discoveries of the age of science. Science, as an activity of analysis, dis-integrates our experience. Poetry integrates. Science splits our experience into fragments—into densities, specific gravities, molecular weights, chemical components, refractive indexes, and conductivity coefficients. Poetry re-affirms the wholeness of experience. Science finds man almost an excrescence in an alien universe: he is an embarrassment in its experiments, and in its results he is seen as a gnat-like creature against the almost limitless immensities of empty space. Poetry re-asserts the primacy of the human being and makes a universe of the human mind and heart. Science enables us to control the outer world: Boom! and we blow up Hiroshima. Poetry enables us to control the inner world—to move men to "thoughts too deep for tears."

Science today is justly proud of having landed men on the moon and begun the process of exploring it. But the poets had been there already and explored it long ago. Homer explored it. Sir Philip Sidney explored it. Keats and Shelley explored it. Edmund Rostand's Cyrano de Bergerac most notably explored it. At a time when no man had yet seen the other side of the moon, Browning told us unforgettably what it was like coming out on that other side:

> But the best is when I glide from out them,
> Cross a step or two of dubious twilight,
> Come out on the other side, the novel
> Silent silver lights and darks undreamed of,
> Where I hush and bless myself with silence.

Yes, the poets long ago explored the moon, and are still exploring it. It is encouraging that here the scientists have at last begun to catch up with them.

But poetry has explored other places that science hasn't even discovered yet. The garden of Eden, the pleasure-dome of Kubla Khan, the Isles of the Blest, Camelot—a city which Tennyson describes as

> built
> To music, therefore never built at all,
> And therefore built forever—

Lilliput, Vanity Fair, Purgatory, Heaven, Hell. Science has been doing a thorough job of exploring the interior of the atom. Poetry, above all, enables us to explore the interior of the heart.

Why poetry in an age of science? To re-affirm the wholeness of experience and the primacy of man; to tell the whole truth about our experience, not just describe its facts; to let us sail on rivers unmapped by any scientist—the inland rivers of the human heart.